SAINTS WITHOUT HALOS

The Human Side of Mormon History

Leonard J. Arrington

and

Davis Bitton

Signature Books

Salt Lake City

Second Printing, 1982

Contents

Introduction

History is often portrayed as the story of movements and their leaders. Typically, historians emphasize key figures who change the course of history by their charismatic personalities, genius, creativity—or simple good fortune. In Latter-day Saint history there has been a tendency to ignore what happens below the top level of administration. The lives of those who drive the engines of history are ignored, often because they leave no written records, but just as often because they are not considered important. Such an attitude is unfortunate, for the vitality and strength of any movement is expressed in the diversity of its experience as well as its unity of purpose.

Mormon history abounds with people of all shapes, sizes, nationalities, and personalities. Their individual stories are not well enough known. Quite apart from the notable lives of the General Authorities there is a wealth of experience in the stories of the members—men and women who, as teachers, bishops, stake presidents, and Relief Society presidents, served faithfully in the vineyards to which they were called.

Historians have a vast reservoir of personal records to tap as they present the human side of Mormon history, as well as the institutional side. When one of the authors compiled *Guide to Mormon Diaries and Autobiographies*, he found nearly three thousand first-hand accounts in public repositories; at least that many more remain virtually unknown in the possession of family members. In this decade alone, thousands of personal histories have been written in response to the counsel of President Spencer W. Kimball. Though many of these will interest only the family of the person keeping the record, many others will certainly interest future historians as they describe the recent expansion of the Church and explore what it means to be a Latter-day Saint in Japan, in Mexico, in Africa—in all parts of the world.

Of the many stories which could be told, we have selected these for their intrinsic value and because they illuminate various facets of our history: early conversion and sacrifice, proselyting, gathering, colonizing, building the kingdom in distant lands, and transforming and modernizing Church programs.

For the most part, these are "mainstream Mormons," Latter-day Saints whose lives reflect the beliefs and values of traditional Mormonism. Only two were General Authorities. All were committed to the restored gospel, although some understood it differently than others. All had their burdens to bear, which they did in their own ways and with varying degrees of success. They are not objects of veneration but human beings who, like the rest of us, struggle to be worthy of the title Latter-day Saint. They are Saints without halos.

Portions of some chapters have appeared in different form in *Arizona and the West*, *BYU Studies*, the *Church News*, the Las Vegas *Sun*, and the *New Era*. We have benefited from the research and editorial work of Scott Kenney and express our appreciation for his help.

1

*From the Beginnings
to the Great Basin*

*T*he first period of Mormon history was not long, but it was exceptionally varied and restless. The main outlines are well known: Joseph Smith's youthful quest for religious certainty and the spiritual manifestations that followed; the coming forth of the Book of Mormon; the organization of the Church in upstate New York; the move to Kirtland, Ohio; the gathering to Missouri; the persecution in both places; the establishment of a new headquarters in Nauvoo, Illinois; the martyrdom of the Prophet; the expulsion from Nauvoo and the trek across the plains to refuge in the Great Basin. Such is the main story line of the Church's first decades.

But there were many subcurrents and side eddies. The missionary net was flung wide and each convert gathered in had his or her own story to tell. Joseph Knight, one of the first to hear the restoration message, came to Joseph Smith's aid when he needed help to continue translating the Book of Mormon, participated in events leading up to the organization of the Church, and became a stalwart in the first branch.

Jonathan Hale, a good example of the first missionaries who spread the gospel message, also played an important role in the move of the "Kirtland Camp" to Missouri; he later assisted the poor to relocate in Illinois and eventually helped supervise the evacuation of Nauvoo.

Lyman Wight, second in command of Zion's Camp, member of the stake presidency in Missouri, fellow-prisoner with the Prophet in Liberty Jail, and finally, apostle, left the main body of the Church and led his own band of followers to Texas. His experience reminds us that people were moving out of the Church as well as coming in. Nine apostles in Joseph Smith's first Quorum of the Twelve were excommunicated, and thousands of others have left the Church for their own reasons, many after having made significant, enduring contributions to the advancement of the gospel.

Thomas Kane, a nonmember, entered the picture just as Lyman Wight was leaving. Touched by the plight of the refugees from Nauvoo, he offered help on many occasions. His intervention on behalf of the Saints in 1857 was especially *crucial and may have been responsible for averting war with the United States.*

One experience shared by most early converts was that of gathering with the Saints. A prominent missionary theme for sixty years, the principle of gathering induced thousands of converts to forsake their homes and move to Missouri, Illinois, and finally to the Great Basin. Between 1849 and 1857 alone, more than 15,000 British converts moved to Utah. One of these was Jean Rio Griffiths Baker. Making the trip as a widow with her seven children in 1851, Jean kept a detailed diary of her ocean voyage and overland trek, giving us an eloquent first-hand account of the experience shared by tens of thousands of nineteenth-century Saints.

Chapter 1

Joseph Knight:
Friend
to the Prophet

In 1811 thirty-nine-year-old Joseph Knight, his wife Polly, and their seven children moved to Colesville, New York, a small rural community on the east bank of the Susquehanna River. They cleared the land, planted an apple orchard, and erected a gristmill. By 1826 the Knights were operating four farms, the area's principal gristmill, and two mills for carding wool.

In connection with these enterprises, Joseph Knight often employed itinerant workers on a seasonal basis. In 1826 Knight's partner in the grain business, Josiah Stowel, recommended Joseph Smith, Jr., from Manchester in western New York. Stowel had engaged the twenty-year-old youth to dig for an old Spanish mine, rumored to be not far from Stowel's farm. But after a month of fruitless effort, Joseph had suggested that Stowel give up the hunt and Stowel, conceding the point but reluctant to put Joseph out of a job, referred the young man to Knight.

Joseph proved to be a good worker. Knight later said that he was "the best hand he ever hired." Also working on the Knight farm were Joseph Knight's sons Newel and Joseph, Jr., ages twenty-five and eighteen, respectively. Joseph roomed with Newel and Joseph, and they became good friends. So close was the relationship between Joseph Smith and the Knight family, that in November 1826 he told them of a sacred event he had experienced at his father's farm: One night in 1823, he had prayed earnestly for forgiveness and sought to know the will of the Lord regarding himself. In the midst of his prayer, he was suddenly visited by a heavenly messenger who introduced himself as Moroni. He told Joseph that ancient records were hidden in a nearby hill. If Joseph remained faithful, the angel said, and if he succeeded in expunging every thought of monetary gain, he would be privileged to translate the records and bring them to the attention of the world. Moroni would visit Joseph once a year for four years. Joseph reported that three of these visits had already occurred, and the last visit would take place on the next September 22.

By the time the promised day arrived, Josiah Stowel and Joseph Knight had joined the Smith family in Manchester. Unfortunately, word of the hidden plates had leaked out, and some nearby residents hoped to find them first, or steal them later from Joseph Smith.

Arising early on the morning of September 22, Joseph Knight noticed that his horse and wagon were gone. Joseph and Emma, his bride of nine months, had borrowed it to go to the hill because no one would recognize it. Soon the young couple returned. Joseph

> turned out the Horse. All Come into the house to Brackfist But no thing said about where they had Bin. After Brackfist Joseph Cald me in to the other Room and he sit his foot on the Bed and leaned his head on his hand and says, well I am Dissopented. Well, say I, I am sorry. Well, says he, I am grateley Dissopnted. It is ten times Better then I expected. Then he went on to tell the length and width and thickness of the plates and, said he, they appear to be gold. But he seamed to think more of the glasses or the urim and thummim than he Did of the plates for says he, I can see anything. They are Marvelous.

During the ensuing months, Joseph Knight followed the translation of the Book of Mormon with keen interest. He offered moral support and provisions, furnishing a pair of shoes, some money, writing paper, a barrel of mackerel, several barrels of grain, "taters," and a pound of tea.

In late March 1830, Joseph Knight drove Joseph to Manchester, New York, to pick up some copies of the Book of Mormon, which had just come off the press. On the way, the Prophet told him that a church must be organized, and a few days later Knight witnessed one of the most moving events of early Mormonism, the baptism of Martin Harris and Joseph Smith, Sr.

> They found a place in a lot a small stream ran thro' and they ware Baptized in the Evening Because of persecution. . . . Joseph was fild with the spirrit to a grate Degree to see his Father and Mr Harris that he Bin with so much he Bust out with greaf and Joy and seamed as tho the world Could not hold him. He went out into the lot and appeared to want to git out of site of every Body and would sob and Crie and seamed to Be so full that he Could not live. Oliver and I went after him and Came to him and after a while he Came in But he was the most wrot upon that I ever saw any man. But his Joy seemed to be full. I think he saw the grate work he had Begun and was Desirus to Carry it out.

Joseph Knight thought about being baptized at the same time, "but I had not red the Book of Morman and I wanted to examin a little more I Being a Restorationar and had not examined so much as I wantd to. But I should a felt Better if I had a gone forward."

Five days later, however, Joseph Knight and son Newel, along with eighteen of their Colesville neighbors, attended the meeting in Fayette where the Church of Christ was organized.

Joseph visited the Knights again in June. This time they were ready to be baptized. A dam was constructed across a nearby stream on Saturday afternoon, but during the night hostile neighbors destroyed it. Oliver Cowdery preached the Sunday sermon and, according to the Prophet's history, "others of us bore testimony to the truth of the Book of Mormon, the doctrine of repentance, baptism for the remission of sins, and laying on of hands for the gift of the Holy Ghost." They repaired the dam and on Monday, Oliver Cowdery baptized thirteen persons, including Joseph's wife Emma, and Joseph and Polly Knight.

7

Before the baptismal service concluded, a mob began to gather. The Saints withdrew to the Knight home, but the mob followed, surrounding the house. When they went to Newel Knight's house, the mob continued to harrass them. "We were obliged to answer them various unprofitable questions," Joseph Smith reported, "and bear with insults and threatenings without number." As evening approached, other Saints began to arrive for a meeting during which the newly baptized members would be confirmed. Before the service could commence, however, a constable entered the house and arrested Joseph Smith "on the charge of being a disorderly person, of setting the country in an uproar by preaching the Book of Mormon, etc."

Joseph Knight employed two lawyers who successfully defended Joseph in the South Bainbridge court the following day. Within an hour of his release, however, Joseph was arrested again—this time on a warrant from neighboring Broome County. Again the two lawyers succeeded in clearing him, although it was after 2:00 A.M. when the defendant was finally released.

Returning with the prophet, Joseph Knight found that neighbors had vandalized his property. Under cover of darkness, they had overturned wagons and piled wood on them, sunk other wagons in water, propped rails against the doors, and sunk chains in the millstream. Nevertheless, Joseph Knight, Jr. reported that when the prophet arrived, "the house was filled with the Holy Ghost which rested on us. . . . It was the greatest time I ever saw."

Colesville became the site of the first branch of the Church. Joseph Knight and his family attended the first Church conferences in June and October 1830. In the fall, Joseph Smith called his brother Hyrum to serve as the Colesville branch president. Hyrum lived for a time with Newel Knight, preaching and baptizing throughout the Susquehanna Valley. In December Orson Pratt, a newly ordained elder from Canaan, New York, was sent on his first mission to labor with Hyrum and Newel in the Colesville area. Among those they baptized was Martin Harris's brother Emer. Emer Harris was the great-grandfather of Franklin Harris, president of Brigham Young University (1921-1945) and of Utah State University (1945-1950); he was also the great-great-grandfather of Dallin Oaks, president of Brigham Young University (1971-1980).

At the third conference of the Church, held in Fayette, New York, on 2 January 1831, Joseph Smith announced a revelation which declared that all members of the Church—now numbering nearly two hundred—should move to Kirtland, in northeastern Ohio. Joseph Knight and the other Colesville members decided to move as a group. They sold their homes, loaded their belongings into three baggage wagons, climbed aboard eleven ox-drawn passenger wagons, and set out for Ohio. At Ithaca, New York, they boarded canal boats and traveled through Cayuga Lake into the Erie Canal. Arriving at Buffalo on 1 May 1831, they were detained by a cold wind which blew ice into the harbor. The party was soon joined by eighty more Church members from Fayette and Waterloo, New York, traveling under the direction of Joseph Smith's mother, Lucy Mack Smith. Together they resumed their journey on an excursion boat to Fairport, Ohio, where they were met by the Prophet Joseph and other Church leaders.

The Colesville group settled sixteen miles northeast of Kirtland on a thousand-acre farm donated by Leman Copley. Joseph Knight and the others consecrated their property, and the bishop assigned stewardships of land, livestock, implements, and other property according to family needs. Those who earned a surplus were asked to consecrate it to the bishop's storehouse to provide for those whose needs exceeded their own resources and to finance community enterprises.

After two months, however, Copley apostatized and sued for the return of his land. The courts, favoring individual property rights, supported Copley's demand, and the Colesville Saints were forced to move.

In twenty-four wagons they traveled to western Missouri, near present-day Independence. As one in the party wrote, "People all along the road stared at us as they would at a circus or a caravan. . . . We most truly were a band of pilgrims started out to seek a better country."

9

Polly Knight's health had been failing for some time, but according to Newel, "she would not consent to stop traveling; her only, or her greatest desire was to set her feet upon the land of Zion, and to have her body interred in that land."

The Colesville branch arrived in Jackson County on 25 July 1831 and began cooperatively to sow grain and build fences and houses. Polly died in just a few days, the first Latter-day Saint to die in Missouri. The Prophet preached her funeral sermon.

Joseph Knight and his son Newel slept in a hen coop while their homes were built, and Newel served as branch president. The Prophet was so impressed with the spirit of unity and service among the Colesville Saints that in 1832 he called them together "and sealed them up to eternal life."

But the same qualities of industry, unity and cooperation which earned them the blessing of the Prophet, aroused the hostility of the "old settler" Missourians. On 1 December 1833 the Mormon settlers were expelled from their homes and farms. Through the winter the Colesville branch huddled together on the Missouri bottom lands of Clay County. Not until 1836 , when they were forced farther north to Caldwell County, did the Colesville branch suspend its practice of the Law of Consecration and Order of Stewardships.

Eventually the Knights moved with the rest of the Saints to Illinois, where they helped build Nauvoo, only to leave it a few years later in the great exodus to the Salt Lake Valley. Joseph and Newel Knight died in Winter Quarters during the winter of 1846-1847. Newel's son Jesse, an important Utah entrepreneur, became one of the Church's most noted benefactors. He employed hundreds of Saints, and his contributions helped save Brigham Young University and the Church itself from financial ruin in the 1890s.

Joseph Smith indicated the great respect he had for Joseph Knight and his family in an 1842 entry made in the Book of the Law of the Lord: "My aged and beloved brother, Joseph Knight, Sen., . . . was among the . . . first to administer to my necessities while I was laboring in the commencement of the bringing forth of the work of the Lord. . . . For fifteen years he has been faithful and true, and even-handed and exemplary, and virtuous and kind. . . . He is a righteous man. . . . [As] a faithful man in Israel, . . . his name shall never be forgotten.'' As for his sons, Newel and Joseph, Jr., the Prophet added, ''I record [their names] in the Book of the Law of the Lord with unspeakable delight, for they are my friends.''

Chapter 2

Jonathan Hale:
Preaching the
Restored Gospel

In 1834 Jonathan Harriman
Hale, a thirty-four-year-old butcher in Dover, New Hampshire, heard the missionaries, and with his wife Olive Boynton Hale, was baptized, as he wrote, "into the New and Everlasting Covenant."

Two months later Jonathan was ordained an elder and set apart to preside over the Dover branch. In the spring, he left Olive and their two children and drove to Bradford, Massachusetts, their former home. There he met two close relatives who had also joined the Church, Henry Harriman and Jonathan Holmes. They drove to Kirtland, Ohio, where they obtained patriarchal blessings from Joseph Smith, Sr., the Church's first Patriarch.

The members of the first Quorum of the Twelve had been called just two months earlier. One of them was John F. Boynton, brother of Jonathan's wife. Perhaps because of that relationship, Jonathan was asked to accompany the Twelve back to New England where they held several conferences.

On May 30 Jonathan and apostles Thomas B. Marsh and David W. Patten visited Martin Harris in Palmyra and climbed the Hill Cumorah, where they "offered up thanks to the most

12

high God for the record of the Nephites and for other blessings." Then they traveled through Palmyra, going "from house to house," and "inquired into the character of Joseph Smith, Jr., previous to his receiving the Book of Mormon." Far from having been the despicable person his detractors had alleged him to be, Joseph was declared by those who knew him to have been "as good as young men in general."

In June, after two months' absence and 1,550 miles of travel, Jonathan returned to his family in Dover. He resumed his work as a butcher for six weeks until he returned to Bradford for a conference of the Twelve. Following the conference, he took three of the Twelve—Thomas B. Marsh, Parley P. Pratt, and Heber C. Kimball—to Salem, Massachusetts, where they had been assigned to labor, and returned to Dover with two other apostles, Luke Johnson and William Smith.

During the following weeks several of the Twelve visited the New Hampshire-Vermont area, and Jonathan took them to their appointments in his buggy. Then he sold his property, settled his business, and moved his family to Bradford for a few months where they lived with Olive's father, Eliphalet Boynton. Jonathan helped him sell his property, and in the spring of 1836 they all moved to Kirtland, "to be with the Saints."

Soon after their arrival Jonathan and Olive arranged for patriarchal blessings for Olive and her relatives. Wilford Woodruff, a friend who would soon become an apostle, baptized their oldest child, Aroet. Many years later Aroet recalled, "My father took the ax along and cut a large hole in the ice. Elder Woodruff got down into the water and baptized me and several other children. My name being Hale, and being baptized in ice water, froze me into the Church and I am still with it, thank God!"

Jonathan worked on the Kirtland Temple and was ordained a seventy. During the winter of 1836-1837 the seventies met every night to study, receive instructions, and conduct ordinances such as washings and anointings.

In May 1837 Jonathan and Wilford were called on a

13

mission. Olive's brother John Boynton laughed out loud when he heard the news and scoffed that it was useless to call such men as Jonathan Hale on a mission, for "he would never baptize a man or make a Mormon." But Jonathan would not be discouraged. During the next five months, while their families lived together, Jonathan and Wilford preached the gospel throughout New York, New England, and eastern Canada.

They walked from farm to farm and village to village, stopping occasionally to bathe in a stream, help a farmer put up hay or butcher a sheep, dig clams, or catch fish. As was the custom, they traveled "without purse or scrip." They preached in barns, homes, schools, town halls, and even in local churches when permitted by the minister. They relied on kind persons to give them lodging for the night or slept in haystacks or under trees.

In each village they preached for two or three days, baptized those who were willing, established a branch, and then moved on to the next village.

At Canton, Connecticut, Jonathan and Wilford preached in the village hall. "As soon as the meeting commenced," Jonathan wrote, "the drums began to beat at the door and continued considerable of the time during the meeting. After the meeting closed, they all gathered round us and appeared like knashing upon us with their teeth." A local minister "said we had no right to cram the people with such doctrine. We told him we didn't cram anybody, but [that] every man had a right to enjoy his opinion. He said they had not if it was wrong. We told him we should take that liberty because the laws of the country gave us that right." After the meeting the two missionaries went to a nearby grove and "offered up our thanks to God for our deliverance."

After another day of fruitless proselyting, "we went by ourselves by a pure stream of water and clensed our hands and feet and bore testimony before God against . . . all that rejected our testimony." Before their mission was over, Jonathan and Wilford washed their feet several more times as a witness that they had attempted to preach the Lord's word and were therefore "washed clean of the sins of these priests of Baal."

14

The most receptive area was the Fox Islands (now Vinal-haven), off the southern coast of Maine. About a thousand people lived in fishing villages on these islands. Several families came forward to be baptized, including a sea captain, Justus Eames, and his wife Betsy. Wilford turned to Jonathan, who had not yet baptized a single person, and said, "Now Brother Hale, we will make John F. Boynton a false prophet. You go down into the sea and baptize this man and woman."

"This was a rejoicing time to us," Jonathan wrote, "and also to them, as I suppose they are the first that has been Baptised into the new and everlasting covenant on the Islands of the sea, (thank the Lord O my soul) and forgit not all his blessings." Two days later the two missionaries retired to a secluded area for a three-hour private service of thanksgiving. Jonathan read Jeremiah 16, "which speaks of fishers and hunters that God will send to gether Israel. We then sung a Song of Zion and offered up our morning prayers to the most high God. We had a glorious time of rejoicing while contemplating our situation—the seanery about us, the work of God. In our prayers we called to mind the ancient apostles Nephi, Mormon, Moroni, Joseph [Smith], Sidney [Rigdon], Oliver [Cowdery], Heber [Kimball], Orson [Hyde], [John] Goodson, and all those in England and . . . Upper Canada, and all in like conditions with our selves, and especially our wives, that God would bless them." Then they wrote letters to their families and "went our way rejoicing."

In the meantime, Olive Hale and Phebe Woodruff missed their husbands and prayed for them morning and night. They were lonely but had little time to brood. They had to provide for their families, plant crops, and take care of business matters. Occasionally they attended lectures and "sings," coped with frequent illnesses, and most importantly, raised the children in the ways of the newly restored gospel. Aroet, who was nine years old while Jonathan was on his mission, recalled, "Sister Phebe Woodruff and mother used to talk to us children and tell us about an angel appearing to the Prophet Joseph when he was a young man, that we must be good children, that angels would not appear to bad children."

Finally, near the end of October 1837 Jonathan and Wilford returned. "Although I have Baptised but nine persons," Jonathan reflected, "I trust my labours are not in vain."

After only two months in Kirtland, Jonathan was called on his second mission, this time to southwestern Ohio and Indiana with Amos B. Fuller. But a few weeks later he received a letter from Olive reporting widespread apostasy. "Brother Joseph Smith, jr., and Sidney Rigdon had fled from Kirtland, for their lives, [and] our enemies had burnt the printing office and takeing many prisoners. Therefore, I felt very anxious to go home."

Jonathan and Amos immediately returned to Kirtland where they found Hyrum Smith and the high council developing a plan to transport the loyal Saints to Missouri by steamboat. When the plan failed to materialize, Jonathan and the other seventies met in the temple to consider their options. According to the minutes of the meeting, "The Spirit of the Lord came down in mighty power and some of the Elders began to prophesy that if the quorum would go up in a body together . . . they should not want for any thing on the journey that would be necessary for them." Then President James Foster arose and "declared that he saw a vision in which was shown unto him a company (he should think of about five hundred) starting from Kirtland and going up to Zion; . . . and that he knew thereby that it was the will of God that the quorum should go up in that manner." Over the next few days a plan was developed for the seventies to combine their resources and move as many as could go to Zion.

Hyrum Smith candidly acknowledged "that what he had said and done in reference to chartering a Steam Boat for the purpose of removing the Church as a body he had done according to his own judgement without any reference to the testimony of the Spirit of God," and advised all the Saints who could to join with the Kirtland Camp.

Jonathan Hale was appointed treasurer and on 5 July 1838 the camp began its 870-mile journey to Far West. The mile-long caravan began with 525 men, women, and children in 59 wagons with 33 large tents. Another hundred people joined the

16

camp along the way. Each morning the bugler sounded the call to arise at 4 A.M., and within twenty minutes all assembled for prayer. Each evening the tents were pitched in the shape of a hollow square. Occasionally the company stopped for a few days while the men worked in local villages chopping wood, making fences, clearing land, and performing other services. Their earnings were given to Jonathan, who bought provisions for the entire camp.

Nevertheless, after a few weeks on the trail, according to the camp recorder, "provisions were scarce and could not be obtained. Consequently we were obliged to do with what we had and here was another manifestation of the power of Jehovah, for seven and a half bushels of corn sufficed for the whole camp consisting of 620 souls for the space of three days and [there was] no lack for food though some complained and mourned because they did not have that to eat that their souls lusted after."

At Mansfield, Ohio, the procession was met by a sheriff and deputies, who took Jonathan and two others into custody for the failure of the Church to pay alleged debts in Kirtland. But the charge could not be substantiated, and they were released the next day.

In late September Jonathan and the other camp members heard reports that Governor Lilburn Boggs had called for volunteers in Missouri to "fight the Mormons." On October 2 Joseph Smith, Sidney Rigdon, and others escorted the Kirtland Camp to the public square at Far West, where they camped for the night.

Two days later, according to the Prophet's history, the camp was temporarily relocated twenty-five miles north of Far West. As the Saints began to pitch their tents, "one of the brethren living in the place proclaimed with a loud voice: 'Brethren, your long and tedious journey is now ended; you are now on the public square of Adam-ondi-Ahman. This is the place where Adam blessed his posterity, when they rose up and called him Michael, the Prince, the Archangel, and he being full of the Holy Ghost predicted what should befall his posterity to the latest generation.' "

Unfortunately, the situation at Adam-ondi-Ahman was not much happier than it had been in Kirtland. On October 27 Governor Boggs issued orders for the state militia to drive the Mormons from the state, and three days later Far West was surrounded. Joseph Smith and other leaders were taken prisoner and mobs began to burn Mormon houses and drive off the livestock. Waiting for assignment to a permanent settlement, the Kirtland Camp, still sheltered only by their tents, suffered from the weather and mob depredations. As winter set in, several died from exposure. "I laid night after night on the Ground with my Brethren, with little or no shelter," Jonathan wrote. "Loaded teams crossed Grand River on the ice. . . . The mobmilitia came in and demanded our arms. We gave them up. We were in number 144, the mob about 800."

Ordered to leave the county within ten days, Jonathan helped apportion the teams, wagons, and other provisions of the well-equipped Saints to assist widows, the aged, the sickly, and the poor. By the end of February two to three thousand Saints had gathered at Quincy, Illinois, where they were generously welcomed by local residents. Jonathan settled his family temporarily in Quincy, looked after the families of other seventies, and in December left on another mission, this time to Illinois and Indiana. He returned two months later, in early 1840 and moved his family to Nauvoo.

Jonathan's leadership abilities had been well established. In Nauvoo he served as bishop, colonel in the Nauvoo Legion, director of schools, collector of donations and tithing for the Nauvoo Temple, and recorder of baptisms for the dead. When the Saints were driven from Nauvoo, he helped direct the exodus.

In Winter Quarters he was sustained as a member of the high council. But strenuous labors drained his energies. With his resistance to disease lowered, Jonathan Hale fell ill and died, probably of typhoid fever, in September 1846. As so often happened during such epidemics, his wife Olive and their two youngest children, Olive and Clarissa, died a few days later.

Four orphaned children remained: Aroet, eighteen; Rachel, seventeen; Alma, ten; and Solomon, seven. Determined to stay together, they remained in Winter Quarters until 1848 when they made the trek across the Great Plains with the Heber C. Kimball division. They remained in the Salt Lake Valley four years, after which Aroet and Alma went to farm in Grantsville, Utah. Rachel married and moved to San Bernardino, California, where she died in 1854. Solomon moved to Farmington, Utah, and in the years that followed, Aroet, Alma, and Sol became Indian fighters, colonizers, missionaries, minute men, stockmen, and operators of sawmills and molasses mills. Two became bishops, one a counselor in the stake presidency, and eventually all three were ordained patriarchs. In the generations since, thousands of Jonathan and Olive's descendants have served as missionaries, ward and stake officers, and productive citizens.

Chapter 3

Lyman Wight:
Wild Ram of the
Mountains

The four Mormon missionaries from New York could hardly have hoped for a more receptive audience than Sidney Rigdon's congregation at Kirtland, Ohio. Hoping for a return to biblical Christianity, they had already formed themselves into a common-stock "Family" patterned along New Testament lines and responded enthusiastically to the missionaries' proclamation of the restoration of Christ's true church on earth. Sidney and many of his followers were soon baptized.

Among the number were Lyman and Harriet Benton Wight—baptized on 14 November 1830. Six days later Lyman and one of the missionaries, Oliver Cowdery, went into the woods about half a mile "and placed ourselves behind a large oak tree. After most solemn prayer he [Oliver] intended to ordain me a priest but he ordained me an elder. He afterwards told me he done it in conformity to a vocal voice."

In a few days Oliver and his companions, Parley P. Pratt, Ziba Peterson, and Peter Whitmer, Jr., resumed their mission to the Indians. In December Sidney and one of his former parishioners, Edward Partridge, traveled to Fayette, New York, to meet Joseph Smith. There the Prophet received a revelation for each of them, converted and baptized Edward, and received another revelation commanding the Saints to gather at Kirtland in the spring. In January Sidney and Edward returned to Kirtland with Joseph Smith, where the prophet received a revelation appointing Edward the first bishop of the Church.

The Colesville and other New York Saints began to arrive in May 1831, and in June a conference was held at which, according to the prophet's history, "the authority of the Melchizedek Priesthood was manifested and conferred for the first time upon several of the Elders." Lyman Wight, who was present, recorded, "I saw the Melchisidek Priesthood introduced into the Church of Jesus Christ as anciently; whereunto I was ordained under the hands of Joseph Smith and I then ordained Joseph and Sidney, and sixteen others such as he chose unto the same priesthood." Among the sixteen others Lyman "ordained to the high Priesthood" were Joseph Smith, Sr., Parley P. Pratt, Thomas B. Marsh, Edward Partridge, Martin Harris, and John Whitmer.

The following day the prophet received a revelation calling Lyman Wight and many others to move to Missouri. Lyman was warned that "Satan desireth to sift him as chaff" but was also promised, "he that is faithful shall be made ruler over many things" (D&C 52:7, 11-12). Lyman left almost immediately; Harriet and their three children joined him in September.

In 1832 he served a five-month proselyting mission to Cincinnati, where he built up a branch of more than one hundred Saints, many of whom returned to Missouri with him.

The influx of large numbers of Mormons disturbed the older settlers. They believed the Mormons were "deluded fanatics" and "the very dregs of . . . society." Mormon revelations were "blasphemous;" their anti-slavery attitude threatened the peace and security of the slave-holders; and, "they declare openly that their God hath given them this country of land, and that sooner or later they must and will have possession of our lands for an inheritance." Fear was so deep and wisdespread that in July several hundred Jackson County residents signed a document expressing their intention "to rid our society, 'peaceably if we can, forcibly if we must,'" of the Mormons. On July 20 they demanded *The Evening and the Morning Star* be discontinued; and when the Saints refused, a mob destroyed the press and nearly all of the Book of Commandments which was being printed. Bishop Partridge and others were tarred and feathered. When the mob reassembled three days later threatening further violence, the Mormon leaders, including Oliver Cowdery, Edward Partridge, W.W. Phelps, and Lyman Wight, promised to leave Jackson County by the first of January 1834, to encourage the other Saints to do likewise, and to cease publication of the *Star*.

In September Lyman and nine others were appointed "to watch over the ten branches of the Church in Zion." In early November word spread through the Mormon settlements that a mob was gathering to storm the jail at Independence, where several Mormons were being held. Lyman, who at the age of seventeen had fought in the War of 1812, quickly assembled a hundred Saints and hurried toward the jail. A mile west of Independence, he was met by Colonel Pitcher of the Missouri militia who demanded their arms. Lyman "agreed that the Church would give up their arms provided the said Colonel Pitcher would take the arms from the mob. To this the Colonel cheerfully agreed." Unfortunately, the mob was not disarmed. The very next day, according to Lyman, they went "from house to house in gangs of from sixty to seventy in number, threatening the lives of women and children if they did not leave [Missouri] forthwith."

The Missouri River was soon lined with twelve hundred Saints fleeing Jackson County. Lyman reported seeing "one hundred and ninety women and children drive thirty miles across the prairie . . . with three decrepit men only in their company; the ground was thinly crusted with sleet, and I could easily follow on their trail by the blood that flowed from their lacerated feet on the stubble of the burnt prairie."

The Saints found refuge in Clay County, and on the first of January 1834 held a conference with Bishop Edward Partridge presiding. Lyman Wight and Parley P. Pratt were delegated to see Joseph Smith in Kirtland and obtain his advice. When Lyman and Parley arrived at Joseph's home in late February, they reported to him and the newly organized high council that

22

the Saints were "comfortable" in Clay County, "but the idea of their being driven away from the land of Zion pained their very souls, and they desired of God, by earnest prayer, to return."

Joseph received a revelation which declared that the Saints would "begin to prevail against [their] enemies from this very hour. And by hearkening to observe all the words which I, the Lord their God, shall speak unto them, they shall never cease to prevail until the kingdoms of the world are subdued under my feet, and the earth is given unto the saints, to possess it forever and ever." Lyman and Parley were commanded not to return home until they had raised a company of men to "redeem Zion." Zion's Camp, with the cooperation of state authorities, was to recover the land in Jackson and provide security for the Saints. Joseph himself would lead the camp. Two days later Joseph and others left to enlist volunteers among the Saints. Lyman and Sidney Rigdon joined them a couple of weeks later in New York.

On the first of May the volunteer army began its trek across Ohio, Indiana, and Illinois. In June Hyrum Smith and Lyman joined the camp with 18 volunteers from Michigan, bringing the total to 205, including 10 women, who served as cooks and washerwomen. Lyman was elected general and made second in command to Joseph.

Soon after they arrived in Missouri, the governor withdrew his pledge of cooperation, and on June 22 Joseph received a revelation that Zion would not be redeemed yet due to the failure of the Church to observe the law of consecration and to support the camp sufficiently.

Included in the revelation was the statement that "I will soften the hearts of the people, as I did the heart of Pharaoh, from time to time, until my servant Baurak Ale [Joseph Smith, Jun.] and Baneemy, whom I have appointed, shall have time to gather up the strength of my house, and to have sent wise men, to fulfill that which I have commanded concerning the purchasing of all the lands in Jackson County that can be purchased . . . for it is my will that these lands should be purchased; and . . . that my saints should possess them according to the laws of consecration which I have given them." According to a letter Lyman Wight later wrote to Wilford Woodruff, Joseph Smith had "blessed and ordained" him "to the office of Baneemy" in Kirtland. The identification of "Baneemy" as "mine elders" was inserted by Orson Pratt in the 1876 edition of the Doctrine and Covenants, when the claims of Lyman Wight no longer seemed relevant. Originally the term appears to have been applied uniquely to Lyman Wight. Lyman believed he had received a specific calling to help lead the Saints to Jackson County at some later date.

In late June a cholera epidemic took several lives. The Saints gathered at Lyman's home near Liberty where Joseph told them that "if they would humble themselves before the Lord and covenant to keep His commandments and obey my counsel, the plague should be stayed from that hour, and there should not be another case of the cholera among them. The brethren covenanted to that effect with uplifted hands, and the plague was stayed."

The next day the leaders again met at Lyman's home where Joseph organized a high council with David Whitmer as president, and W.W. Phelps and John Whitmer as assistant presidents. Lyman Wight, Thomas B. Marsh, and Parley P. and Orson Pratt were among the twelve councilors. Lyman and the other members of Zion's Camp had been tried, tested, and found worthy of important responsibilities.

In the summer of 1834 Lyman contracted to build a large brick house for a local resident. Wilford Woodruff was among those who helped Lyman make the 100,000 bricks needed.

In the fall of 1835 Lyman returned to Kirtland, where he attended the School of the Prophets for two and a half months and received his washings and anointings prior to the dedication of the Kirtland Temple. He also received a patriarchal blessing from Joseph Smith, Sr., which warned him that Satan would "try to lift thee up in pride and make thee think much of thy self for thy eloquence;" but he was also promised that if he remained faithful he would have power to prevail; he would call thousands into the fold and would live to see "many people visited with the wrath and indignation of the most High, because they reject the fullness of the gospel."

24

Lyman's home was situated at the foot of a hill which in May 1838, the Prophet named " 'Tower Hill' . . . in consequence of the remains of an old Nephite altar or tower that stood there." Nearby Spring Hill he renamed Adam-ondi-Ahman because "it is the place where Adam shall come to visit his people." Lyman's home served as headquarters for the surveying teams and early settlers of Adam-ondi-Ahman. When a stake was organized, Joseph called Lyman to be President John Smith's second counselor.

As Latter-day Saints began arriving in large numbers, the old-time settlers became apprehensive and tensions mounted. In mid-October Mormon homes at Adam-ondi-Ahman and elsewhere in Daviess County were burned. As a colonel in the Missouri militia, Lyman immediately raised a force to disperse the mob. Members of the mob claimed that Lyman was leading a "Danite" band that burned their homes and committed other depredations, but Lyman insisted the Missourians had burned their own cabins in order to discredit the Saints.

On October 27 Governor Boggs ordered the Missouri militia to treat the Mormons as "enemies" who "must be exterminated or driven from the state, if necessary for the public good." Three days later, two hundred militiamen attacked the tiny Mormon settlement of Haun's Mill and massacred seventeen inhabitants. The next day, the militia advanced on Far West and demanded the Saints surrender. On the pretext of negotiating a peaceful settlement, Colonel George Hinckle lured Joseph Smith, Sidney Rigdon, Lyman Wight, Parley P. Pratt, and George W. Robinson into the militia's camp and promptly arrested them. The following day Hyrum Smith and Amasa Lyman were taken prisoner. When one of the militia's generals tried to induce Lyman to testify against Joseph, he reportedly replied, "You are entirely mistaken. . . . Joseph Smith . . . is as good a friend as you have got. Had it not been for him, you would have been in hell long ago, for I should have sent you there, by cutting your throat, and no other man but Joseph Smith could have prevented me, and you may thank him for your life. And now, if you will give me the boys I brought from Diahman yesterday, I will whip your whole army." Informed that he would be shot at 8 A.M., Lyman declared, "Shoot and be damned."

Fortunately, General Alexander Doniphan indignantly refused to carry out the execution order, calling it "cold-blooded murder." Instead, the prisoners were taken to Richmond where they were tried on charges of high treason, murder, burglary, arson, robbery, and larceny. At the end of November Joseph and Hyrum Smith, Sidney Rigdon, Lyman Wight, Alexander McRae, and Caleb Baldwin were remanded to the jail at Liberty.

For four and a half months Lyman and the others languished in their twenty-two-foot-square prison. The upper room was dimly lit by two small windows while the dungeon had no light at all. The food was "so filthy we could not eat it until we were driven to it by hunger." The inhumane conditions seemed to bond Lyman to Joseph Smith. He was one of the five who signed the inspiring letters later canonized as Sections 121-123 of the Doctrine and Covenants. He was also present when Joseph Smith III was brought to the jail and the Prophet blessed his six-year-old son. Finally, the case became such an embarrassment to the state that the prisoners were allowed to escape in April.

When Lyman arrived in Illinois, he settled his family temporarily in Nauvoo, served a mission to the East, and then in 1839 moved to Augusta, Iowa, where he served as a counselor to stake president John Smith.

At the April 1841 conference, Sidney Rigdon nominated Lyman to fill the vacancy in the Council of the Twelve caused by the death of Elder David W. Patten. Nine of the Twelve were in England at the time and did not learn of the appointment until they returned in the summer. In the meantime, Lyman was assigned to "travel and collect funds" for the Nauvoo Temple.

He was also appointed a member of the three-man committee responsible for building the Nauvoo House. The revelation calling him to the position promised that the Lord would "bear him as on eagles' wings; and he shall beget glory and honor to himself and unto my name. That when he shall

26

finish his work I may receive him unto myself." Lyman returned to his activities with renewed energy. In 1842 he rebaptized two hundred Kirtland Saints and brought many to Nauvoo.

In 1843 he was appointed to head a Wisconsin logging operation that would provide lumber for the temple and Nauvoo House. While he was there, Joseph and the Twelve considered alternative sites to Nauvoo for settlement. Lyman and George Miller recommended Texas. Joseph authorized Lyman to lead a company to Texas; but before the expedition could be arranged, he and other members of the new Council of Fifty were sent east to campaign for Joseph Smith as president of the United States.

Lyman, Brigham Young, and Heber C. Kimball campaigned in Saint Louis, Cincinnati, and Pittsburgh. William Smith, Lyman, and Heber petitioned government leaders in Washington, D.C., for remuneration of the Church's losses in Missouri, and visited Wilmington, Delaware, and Philadelphia, Pennsylvania, William Smith's home.

In Philadelphia Lyman found nearly two hundred Saints, "out of which number many have commenced sickening, and were growing faint at the many false reports in circulation, fearing that the Prophet had fallen and the Twelve were in transgression. . . . We shall call on them to know whether they intend to gather with the living and sustain the cause of God . . . or die in Philadelphia. If they should choose the latter, we shall attend to the funeral ceremonies, and leave them to rest with the dead, and we will go our way among the living." Two days later the Philadelphia branch voted to sustain the First Presidency and the Twelve, as did the Wilmington conference, which also voted to "go whithersoever the Presidency, Patriarch and Twelve want, should it be to Oregon, Texas, or California, or any other place."

Lyman was in Baltimore when he heard the news that Joseph and Hyrum had been murdered. He met Brigham and Heber in Boston; they were joined in Albany by Orson Hyde, Orson Pratt, and Wilford Woodruff. Lyman hurried on to Nauvoo, arriving on July 31, a few days ahead of his brethren.

27

On Wednesday, August 7 Lyman and seven other apostles met at John Taylor's house in Nauvoo, where they found him recovering from the wounds he had received at Carthage Jail. Later that afternoon Sidney Rigdon called upon a group of leaders to accept himself as "guardian" of the Church, but they sustained Brigham Young's declaration that the Twelve should lead the Church. The procedure was repeated the next day at a general meeting of the Church membership.

Lyman addressed the Saints on Sunday about taking a company "into the wilderness." On Monday the Twelve voted "that Brigham Young, Heber C. Kimball, and Willard Richards . . . manage the general affairs of the Church; that Lyman Wight go to Texas as he chooses, with his company." But the following Sunday, August 18, Brigham Young condemned the "disposition in the sheep to scatter, now the shepherd is taken away. . . . There is no man who has any right to lead away one soul out of this city by the consent of the Twelve, except Lyman Wight and George Miller, they have had the privilege of taking the 'Pine Company' where they pleased, but not another soul has the consent of the Twelve to go with them. . . . I tell you in the name of Jesus Christ that if Lyman Wight and George Miller take a course contrary to our counsel and will not act in concert with us, they will be damned and go to destruction."

On August 24 the Twelve counseled Lyman to "go north instead of going south." He returned to Wisconsin and prepared his camp for the move to Texas. He wrote relatives that he wanted to go to a land that would never be "defiled by Gentile customs and practices."

Lyman's camp spent the winter in tents. When spring arrived, they started down the Mississippi River in four homemade boats. Impoverished, they were forced to sell some of their clothes, including Lyman's only coat, to buy food. In April 1845 the Twelve wrote, counseling them "in the name of the Lord . . . not to go west at present. We desire, dear brethren, that you should take hold with us and help us to accomplish the building of the Lord's houses. Come brethren, be one with us, and let us be agreed in all of our exertions to roll on the great wheel of the kingdom." But Lyman would not abandon his dream, and continued on through Iowa and Kansas. In August W.W. Phelps wrote a newspaper article that identified Brigham Young as "The Lion of the Lord" and—just as appropriately—Lyman Wight as "The Wild Ram of the Mountains."

On November 10 Lyman and his hundred and fifty followers crossed the Red River into Texas, first settling in the ruins of old Fort Johnson (Georgetown). In the spring of 1846 they moved south to Austin, but it was "settling fast," Lyman's son recalled, "and it was soon feared that we would be crowded and that, too, by slave holders." So in 1847 the colony moved eighty miles west to a site on the Pedernales River where they began a communitarian settlement called Zodiac. The following year they were joined by George Miller and a few others.

Lyman published a lengthy justification of his independent course entitled *An Address by way of an Abridged Account and Journal of My Life from February 1844 up to April 1848*, emphasizing his ordination "from him who then stood, and who now stands at the head of the Church of Jesus Christ of Latter Day Saints," and insisting he had not forfeited his right "to a seat with the Twelve, neither with the Grand Council [Council of Fifty]." He longed for the day that God would call for the building of the temple in Zion, Jackson County, Missouri, for then the "Grand Council of heaven" would launch "a mighty mission in the earth," and bring forth "their thousands and their tens of thousands to the help of Zion."

Brigham Young sent representatives to persuade Lyman to come to Salt Lake City. But, they reported, he told them that "nobody under the light of heavens except Joseph Smith or [Patriarch] John Smith, the president of the Fifty, could call him from Texas to Salt Lake City, and that he had as much authority to call one of the Twelve, or rather Eleven, to Texas, as they had to call him to Salt Lake City."

In December 1848 Lyman was disfellowshipped and later excommunicated. His followers built a "temple" at Zodiac and performed foot washings, body washings, anointings, and baptisms for the dead. They practiced a form of consecration and stewardship, and plural marriage. Later they recognized William Smith (Joseph's younger brother) as president of the Church with Lyman as his counselor until Joseph Smith III became leader of the Reorganized Church of Jesus Christ of Latter Day Saints.

When a flood washed out the mill dam, the colony moved to Hamilton's Creek, then to the Medina River, and finally, to Mountain Valley (1854). Defections steadily reduced the colony's numbers. In 1858 Lyman gathered the straggling remnant of his colony and started for Jackson County, but died in central Texas.

Lyman Wight's movement quickly collapsed. Mormonism in the West was following pragmatic leaders who were determined to build up Zion in the Rocky Mountains while scattered Saints in Illinois, Iowa, and Missouri were starting to band together in what became the eminently respectable but scarcely apocalyptic Reorganization. Mormonism's wild ram was fortunate in dying when he did, true to his own guiding vision, his eyes fixed on the alabaster walls of the New Jerusalem.

Chapter 4

Colonel Thomas L. Kane: A Friend in Need

The great migration of Latter-day Saints to the Rocky Mountains began in the spring of 1846. Under the direction of Brigham Young, sixteen thousand Saints traveled overland, while several hundred living along the Atlantic seaboard planned to sail around Cape Horn and on to Yerba Buena (now San Francisco) under the leadership of Samuel Brannan.

Elder Jesse C. Little, who replaced Samuel Brannan as leader of the Church in the eastern states, was directed to contact government officials in Washington, D.C., to see if they would provide any assistance for the migration.

On 13 May 1846 Jesse Little addressed a special conference of the Church in Philadelphia. In attendance was a twenty-four-year-old nonmember, Thomas L. Kane. Thomas was a son of John Kintzing Kane, a prominent federal judge. He had attended school in Philadelphia, England, and France. Among his teachers had been Auguste Comte, the founder of modern sociology. Upon his return to the United States, Thomas served as law clerk to his father and was admitted to the bar. He read newspaper accounts of the Mormons in Illinois, their forced flight from Nauvoo, and their trek across Iowa. Kane's humanitarian impulses were stirred, though he later confessed that he also saw in "the Mormon problem" an opportunity to advance his own political career. When he read of Jesse Little's intention to address the Philadelphia conference, Thomas decided to attend.

After the morning session Thomas invited the Mormon home, where they talked for several hours. Jesse spoke of the exodus from Nauvoo, the voyage of the *Brooklyn* to California, and his hopes for obtaining assistance from the federal government. Thomas wrote a letter of introduction for him to the vice-president of the United States. In return, Jesse prepared a letter to introduce Thomas to Brigham Young.

Jesse visited the vice-president and other federal officials in Washington. Then, early in June, Thomas joined him, and together they called upon President James K. Polk and lobbied for government assistance. The Polk administration agreed to enlist a battalion of five hundred Mormons for the campaign to take the West from Mexico. The Mormon Battalion would travel as part of the Army of the West from Fort Leavenworth, Kansas, to San Diego, California. Thus, the government would provide transportation for the five hundred men and a few Mormon women who would work as laundresses and cooks. Their pay in gold would help purchase provisions and equipment for the families who would come west later.

Upon completion of the negotiations, Thomas and Jesse traveled to St. Louis. Jesse went to Nauvoo and Thomas continued on, delivering secret dispatches from President Polk and the secretary of war to General Kearney at Fort Leavenworth. As soon as he received his orders, Kearney dispatched Captain James Allen to begin recruiting men for the battalion among the Mormon camps in Iowa.

Thomas went to the temporary Mormon settlement, later named Kanesville, and still later Council Bluffs, Iowa, on the bluffs overlooking the Missouri River. Shortly after his arrival, Thomas, never physically robust, contracted pulmonary tuberculosis and nearly died. During his long convalescence, he often strolled through the woods, visited with the Saints, and watched them prepare for the western trek. Occasionally he was joined by Henry G. Boyle, a member of the Battalion who had not yet departed. Boyle wrote that one day he and Thomas heard someone "praying in secret in the skirt of the woods, in the rear of one of our camps. It seemed to affect [Kane] deeply, and as we walked away he observed that our people were a praying people, and that was evidence enough to him that we were sincere and honest in our faith."

Thomas attended the farewell ball honoring those who had joined the Battalion, noting that women had donated their gold earrings to the common purse and men had sold their "useless pocket watches" to buy wagons and supplies.

Hardship, hunger, and death were common among the Latter-day Saint refugees, but to Thomas's amazement he also found a spirit of love and faith. The tender care he received from the Saints who nursed him back to health, and their sincerity and devotion to God made a deep impression on him. "I believe there is a crisis in the life of every man," he later wrote his Mormon friends, "when he is called upon to decide seriously and permanently if he will die unto sin and live unto righteousness. . . . Such an event, I believe, . . . was my visit to [the Mormon camps on the Missouri]. It was the spectacle of your noble self denial and suffering for conscience sake [that] first made a truly serious and abiding impression upon my mind, commanding me to note that there was something higher and better than the pursuit of the interest of earthly life for the spirit made after the image of Deity."

During the summer of 1846 Thomas helped to secure the consent of the Pottawatomi Indians for the Saints to occupy part of their lands. Then, though he was not a member of the Church, he requested Church Patriarch John Smith to give him a blessing on 7 September 1846. It assured him that "the Lord is well pleased with your exertions. He has given His angels charge over you to guard you in times of danger, to help you in time of trouble, and to defend you from your enemies. Not a hair of your head will fall by the hand of an enemy. For you are called to do a great work on the earth and you shall be blessed in all your undertakings. Your name shall be had in honorable remembrance among the Saints to all generations."

Deeply moved, Thomas committed himself to be a sincere

friend of the Latter-day Saints, their "second in an affair of honor," as he put it. For the remainder of his life Thomas Kane was identified with the "vindication and defense" of the Latter-day Saints.

Returning to Philadelphia, he stopped off in Nauvoo to witness with his own eyes the sad consequences of the anti-Mormon agitation there. When he reached Washington, D.C., he reported what he had seen to President Polk. Then he traveled throughout the eastern cities trying to correct popular misconceptions about the Latter-day Saints.

In the years that followed, he often wrote the president of the United States about "the Mormon situation," lobbied cabinet officers and members of Congress, talked to influential newspaper editors, and regularly sent advice and encouragement to Church leaders in the Great Basin.

He suggested the formation of the state of Deseret and sought congressional approval for its recognition. Campaigning for recognition of Deseret as a state, he addressed the Historical Society of Pennsylvania on the subject of the Mormons. His stirring address was published as an eighty-four-page pamphlet and sent to the president, cabinet members, senators, congressmen, editors, and other prominent men in Washington.

Even though a territorial government was established instead of a state, the Saints were immensely grateful for Thomas's help. They sent him a specially made wolfskin sleigh robe and some of the gold which the Mormon Battalion members brought back from California. Thomas had the gold made into seal rings for Horace Greeley and others who assisted in the vindication of the Mormons, and one ring each for Brigham Young, Heber C. Kimball, and Willard Richards. He gave the sleigh robe to his brother Elisha Kane when he left to search for Sir John Franklin, lost in the Arctic ice. The robe, Thomas wrote to Brigham Young, "may be only the more honored by being the first missionary of Mormonism to the North Pole."

The Saints so appreciated their eastern advocate that they offered to elect him their delegate to Congress, but he declined, saying he could do no more for the people as an independent agent.

Thomas Kane's most important service to the Latter-day Saints occurred during the so-called Utah War. President James Buchanan had received reports from three federal officials who had served in Utah that the Mormons were in a state of rebellion. They charged that federal court records had been destroyed, that Mormons openly interfered with the mail service, and that government officials were fearful for their lives.

Without any investigation, Buchanan ordered 2,500 troops to Utah to install a new governor and other territorial officials, by force if necessary. No official notice was sent to Governor Brigham Young or to the residents of Utah Territory.

The Utah Expedition left Fort Leavenworth in the summer of 1857. A number of Saints en route to the Salt Lake Valley observed the troops, infiltrated their companies, and learned that they were headed for Utah "to scalp old Brigham," "massacre Mormon leaders," and "drive the hated Mormons from their homes." Realizing the danger, the Mormons drove their horses as hard as they could and arrived in the Valley on the afternoon of 24 July 1857. Brigham Young and the Saints were in nearby Big Cottonwood Canyon celebrating the tenth anniversary of their entrance into the valley.

Remembering their experiences in Missouri and Illinois, Brigham Young and his associates considered the troops to be a federal militia on its way to exterminate the Mormons. The Saints hurriedly armed, dispatched an army to eastern Utah, and prepared for the worst. Mormon raiders slowed the movement of the federal troops by burning their supply wagons and capturing their cattle and horses. The Mormon tactics were so effective that Colonel Albert Sidney Johnston, who commanded the troops, ordered his expedition to "hole up" at Fort Bridger in southwestern Wyoming for the winter of 1857-1858.

Meanwhile, Thomas Kane began to intercede on behalf of the Saints. He wrote or talked to his many newspaper friends, contacted political acquaintances, and wrote President

Buchanan, recounting the harsh treatment the Mormons had received from the government since the time of the Missouri persecutions.

It seemed that only the intervention of a person respected by both sides could avoid bloodshed. When Thomas Kane offered his services as a mediator, Buchanan thanked him for his willingness to abandon the comforts of friends, family, and home, and go to Utah at his own expense. The president wrote Thomas that he had his confidence but no official status, and was "recommended to the favorable regard of all the officers of the United States whom he would meet as he traveled."

In January Thomas left New York on a steamer. He appropriated the name of his black servant and traveled as Dr. A. Osborne, botanist with the Academy of Natural Sciences of Philadelphia. They disembarked at Panama, crossed the isthmus, sailed up the California coast, and hurried on to the Mormon community of San Bernardino. There they were assisted by two Mormon families who arranged transportation and provisions for "Dr. Osborne" and his servant.

Kane arrived in Salt Lake City on 25 February 1858 and immediately conferred with Church leaders. Brigham Young's journal describes the meetings as follows: "Colonel Kane . . . tried to point out a policy for me to pursue. But I told him I should not turn to the right or to the left, or pursue any course except as God dictated. . . . When he found that I would be informed only as the Spirit of the Lord led me, he was at first discouraged. Then he said, I could dictate, he would execute. I told him that as he had been inspired to come here, he should go to the Army and do as the Spirit of the Lord led him, and all should be right. He did so and all was right."

When the conversation turned to Kane's health, President Young said, "The Lord has sent you here, friend Thomas, and He will not let you die, No, you cannot die until your work is done. Your name will live with the Saints in all eternity. You have done a great work, and you will do a greater work still."

About ten days after his arrival in Salt Lake City, Thomas started for the army camps in Wyoming, accompanied by a Mormon escort. As he neared the camps, he dismissed the escort and rode on alone. He arrived exhausted, and the soldiers had to take him from his horse. He insisted on transacting his business with the newly appointed governor, Alfred Cumming. Thomas argued earnestly and persuaded Governor Cumming that he would be recognized as governor by the Saints, that the court records had not been burned, that the Mormons were not in a state of rebellion, and that the army should not be allowed to remain in the Salt Lake Valley.

Negotiations with the army leaders were not so pleasant. One officer shot at Thomas, missing him narrowly. Colonel Johnston dispatched an orderly to invite Thomas to dinner, but instead, the orderly arrested him. Fortunately, the affair blew over quickly, when Thomas was informed that Johnston had not ordered the arrest.

In April Thomas and Governor Cumming left the army camp to meet with Brigham Young in Salt Lake City. The new governor quickly recognized that the charges against the Mormons were not true and that he would indeed be recognized as governor. After his "final and decisive" interview with Alfred Cumming on April 24 a gratified Thomas Kane wrote in his diary, "I am and know myself to be happy."

His mission accomplished, Thomas returned to Washington and reported to President Buchanan, who arranged to have the Mormons "pardoned" and to have the army stationed no closer than forty miles from Salt Lake City. It was a great personal triumph for Thomas; he had accomplished everything he had desired. In his next annual message to Congress, Buchanan paid special tribute to Kane: "I cannot refrain from mentioning . . . the valuable services of Colonel Thomas L. Kane, who from motives of pure benevolence, and without any official character or pecuniary compensation, visited Utah during the last inclement winter for the purpose of contributing to the pacification of the territory."

The tribute from the Latter-day Saints was even more glowing: "You were an instrument in the hands of God," wrote Wilford Woodruff, "and you were inspired by Him to turn away. . . the edge of the sword, saving the effusion of much blood, and performing what the combined wisdom of the nation could not accomplish, changing the whole face of affairs, with effects which will remain forever."

After distinguishing himself in the Civil War, Major General Thomas Kane took his family to begin developing land in McKean County, Pennsylvania. He opened roads, built railroads, and in a few years became financially independent. A succession of Mormon missionaries and envoys visited him regularly and were treated as "family."

At the invitation of Brigham Young, Thomas brought his family to Utah for the winter of 1872-73. When he returned to Philadelphia, Thomas prepared a will for Brigham Young and drafted other documents to found the Brigham Young College in Logan, the Brigham Young Academy, and the Young University (later absorbed into the University of Utah) in Salt Lake City.

When Brigham Young died in 1877, General Kane characteristically dropped everything and hurried to Salt Lake City to express his sorrow and to assure himself that the Mormon cause would continue to prosper. After meeting with President John Taylor and members of the Twelve, he observed "The Lord has made ample provision for the preservation of that cause which lies near to my heart."

On 26 December 1883, at the age of sixty-one, Thomas Kane died of pneumonia at his Philadelphia home. A letter from his wife to George Q. Cannon describes his last moments:

"Your friend suffered intensely until a few hours of his release, his mind was wandering from the outset of the attack. Yet in the intervals of consciousness he was fully persuaded of the approach of death, and made efforts to give us counsel and bid us farewell. In one of these lucid moments he said: 'My mind is too heavy, but do send the sweetest message you can make up to my Mormon friends—*to all my dear Mormon friends*.' Nothing I could make up," she wrote, "could be sweeter to you than this evidence that you were in his last thoughts."

Chapter 5

Jean Baker: Gathering to Zion

At the age of forty-one, Jean Rio Griffiths Baker was about to embark on the greatest journey of her life. She opened her diary and began to write. "January 4, 1851. I am now, with my children, about to leave forever my native land in order to gather with the Church of Christ in the Valley of Great Salt Lake in North America."

She had been a widow for a year and a half. Six sons and one daughter, ages four to seventeen, depended on her. Gathering to Zion semed to be the most important thing she could do for them and for herself.

So Jean and her children boarded the *George W. Bourne* in London, bound for New New Orleans. The ship was towed into the river, her sails ready to catch the first favorable winds—which did not rise for twelve days.

In the meantime, the Mormon emigrants organized themselves with Elder William Gibson, a Scotsman, as branch president, and divided up their provisions according to need.

Finally the winds picked up and carried the *Bourne* quickly out to sea. During the first two days, one of the Mormon women delivered a baby boy and Elder Gibson married a couple. Porpoises played around the ship, while the passengers enjoyed the calm waters and warm sunshine.

After a month at sea Jean again turned to her diary to record her feelings. "I can hardly describe the beauty of this night," she wrote. "The moon nearly at full with a deep blue sky studded with stars, the reflection of which makes the sea appear like an immense sheet of diamonds. . . . Well I have seen the mighty deep in its anger, with our ship nearly on her beam ends, and I have seen it, as now, under a cloudless sky, and scarcely a ripple on its surface, and I know not which to admire most. . . . I feel most powerfully the force of those words, The Mighty God, which Handel has so beautifully expressed in one of his Chronicles."

But the world Jean admired so much for its great beauty also contained much sorrow. When they left England, Jean prayed that the sea air would restore the health of her four-year-old Josiah. But he continued to sink and on February 22 breathed his last. "When witnessing his sufferings I have prayed that the Lord would shorten them. He has done so and my much loved child is now in the world of spirits, awaiting the morning of the Resurrection. . . . The Captain has given me permission to retain his little body until tomorrow, when it will be committed to the deep, nearly a thousand miles from land."

Her faith in God and the encouragement of fellow Saints helped assuage Jean's grief. The sun continued to rise every day, her other children still needed her attention, and the journey had only begun.

A bugle sounds every morning to let us know it is six o'clock, when all arise. At half past seven it sounds again for morning prayer, after which, breakfast. Sometimes a few musical ones get together and have a few tunes, sometimes [we] sit down and gossip, and so the days pass along. When we have rough weather we have enough to do to keep on our feet, and laugh at those who are not so clever as ourselves. . . . Our general custom is to sit on the deck and take our meals on our laps. Each family have their own department in front of their berths and can have their meals without being intruded on by others. . . . Our president, William Gibson, is to watch over us as a pastor, to counsel, exhort, reprove if necessary; in short, to see that all our doings are in accordance with our profession as Saints of the most high God.

Approaching the Bahamas, the *Bourne* encountered heavy squalls. "It was awful, yet grand, to look upon the sea," Jean wrote. "I could only compare it to the boiling of an immense cauldron covered with white foam, while the roaring of the winds and waves was like the bellowing of a thousand wild bulls."

On March 12 the *Bourne* reached the Gulf of Mexico. But the excitement of the sea-weary Saints was dampened by the excommunication of two sisters "for levity of behavior with some of the officers of the ship and continued disregard of the counsels of the President."

A week later Jean and the other passengers transferred to a steamer which took them up the Mississippi, past grand plantations, orange groves, and peach and plum trees in blossom. Flocks of wild geese flew overhead, while foxes and racoons were spotted along the river banks. "The only thing which detracts from its beauty," she wrote, "is the sight of hundreds of negroes at work in the sun. Oh! Slavery how I hate thee."

In New Orleans Jean and her children stayed with Mrs. Blime, the sister of a friend, who took them to a slave auction:

It is a large hall, well lighted, with seats all round on which were girls of every shade of colour, from 10 or 12 to 30 years of age and to my utter astonishment they were singing as merrily as larks. I expressed my surprise to Mrs. Blime and she said "Though I am an English woman, detest the very idea of slavery, yet I do believe that many of the slaves here have ten times the comforts of many of the laborers in our own country with not half the labor. I have been 13 years in this country and although I have never owned a slave, or intend to do so, still I do not look upon slavery with the horror that I once did. There are hundreds of slaves here who would not accept their freedom if it was offered to them. For this reason they would then have no protection, as the laws afford little or none to people of color." I could not help thinking that my friend's feeling had become somewhat blunted, if not hardened by long residence in Slave States.

After visiting New Orleans, the Bakers boarded the river-boat *Concordia* for Saint Louis, a trip of 1,250 miles that took six days. Saint Louis was a boom town, frequently used by

Mormon immigrants as a stopping off place where they could rest and regroup for the overland journey. The city's rapid growth afforded employment opportunities which many needed to earn provisions for the final leg of their journey.

At Saint Louis, Jean rented a two-bedroom house for a month. The first evening in her new home a man came to the door and introduced himself as "Brother Howard," a member of the Church. During the next few weeks Brother and Sister Howard helped Jean and her family adjust to their temporary home. Their children played together and on Sundays they attended the Mormon services in the concert hall on Market Street. One week Jean was amazed to find the 3,000-seat hall "filled to overflowing and the staircase and lobby crowded with those who could not get inside." The branch even had its own orchestra and a good choir.

But Jean's ultimate destination was still the Salt Lake Valley. She purchased eight yoke of oxen and four wagons, and on April 19 boarded the steamboat *Financier* for Alexandria, Missouri. Barges were lashed to both sides of the steamer, one for wagons, the other for cattle. Jean and her family waived their right to berths in the *Financier* to remain with the wagons, where they could sleep in comfort, free from the constant jerking caused by the steamboat's machinery.

At Alexandria Jean's family did their first camping out. When they had made a fire, watered and fed the cattle, and made their beds in the wagons, they huddled together and "unitedly offered up our thanksgivings to the God of Heaven for bringing us here in safety, through unseen and unknown danger, and then retired to rest, feeling sure of His protection during the night."

Soon they were making their way across Iowa. "Do not expect me to describe our road, as they call it," Jean wrote in irritation. "It is a perfect succession of hills, valleys, bogs, mudholes, low bridges, quagmires with stumps of trees a foot above the surface of the watery mud, so that without the utmost care, the wagons should be overturned ten times a day. Oh for the Town Roads of Old England."

Such conditions led to accidents or damage to almost every wagon in the company. When one of Jean's wagons became

42

stuck, the sudden yank meant to dislodge it broke the tongue pin. They decided to stop for the night and soon had a fire and kettle on. "While we were preparing our supper, a farmer-looking man accompanied by a tall, well-looking negro came up and offered to assist us in repairing our wagon, and setting to work at once, in about two hours all was right again. The farmer then bade us good night, refusing all recompence and taking two of the lads in order that they might bring back a supply of corn for our cattle." Meanwhile, the "black visitor" remained for supper and entertained the camp until midnight with his tales of Indian wars.

Jean and her companions were favorably impressed with Iowans.

> Nothing can exceed the kindness of the people as we pass along. Many a time when our wagons have been in a mud hole, the men working in the fields have left their plow to come and help us out. Men, too, who in our country would be called gentlemen, owning 500 to 1,000 acres of land. But it seems to be a rule among them to help everyone who is in need and they are ready at all times to impart any information which they think will be useful to us. Their wives are just the same. We try to encamp near a farmhouse for the convenience of supplying ourselves with butter, eggs, and milk. We are sure to be invited to their houses in order to partake of the hospitality.

She was delighted with the variety of flowers growing on the prairies. "We are constantly walking over violets, prim-roses, daisies, bluebells, the lilly of the valley, columbines of every shade, from white to the deepest purple, Virginia stocks in large patches. The wild rose, too, is very plentiful, perfuming the air for miles." But flowers did not entirely compensate for the tedious travel, quagmires, broken wagons, and accidents in which wagons ran over women or children. In the first thirty-two days out of Alexandria they had traveled only 116 miles.

Occasionally, there were terrible thunder and rain storms. Once when she went to a farm house a mile away in search of butter,

> heavy rains came on so that I could not return to the camp, the water being in the hollows higher than my knees. I have stayed all

43

night at the farm house. The thunder has been fearful. It seemed even to have frightened the wolves, who have been howling and yelping around the house all night. We have had thunderstorms every day for four weeks. . . . I cannot describe the thunder. It is unlike any I have ever heard. As to the rain upon our wagon covers, I can only compare it to millions of shot falling on sheets of copper. Sleep is out of the question as well as conversation, for though Aunt and I were in the same wagon it was with difficulty we could make each other hear.

With rain almost every day, they encountered many swollen streams and inundated bottomlands. They put seven or eight yokes of oxen to each wagon to pull it through the mud, stopping every few minutes for the animals to recover their breath.

Finally, on July 2, they arrived at Kanesville (now Council Bluffs, Iowa). Jean found it a pretty town and the surrounding scenery beautiful. "And there was a good omen," she wrote. "I heard a whippoorwill this evening."

Four days later, their company of fifty-four wagons was organized for crossing the Plains. John Brown, an experienced frontiersman, was captain.

As they neared Fort Kearney, Nebraska, one of Jean's finest oxen fell down and died in just a few minutes. Fortunately, she was able to buy another two days later for $30.

As they crossed the Platte, Captain Brown passed the word for all wagons to keep as close together as possible. They were in Indian territory. Soon they were greeted by

ninety of the principal warriors with their families, going to a great council of various tribes, to endeavor to settle their differences and bury the tomahawk. They made a grand appearance, all on horseback and gaily dressed. Some with lances, others with guns or bows and arrows, also a number of ponies carrying their tents, and the men passed on one side of us and the women and children on the other, but all of them well mounted. Their clothing was beautiful, trimmed with small beads. Altogether it was quite an imposing procession.

When she reached the Rocky Mountains, Jean wrote, "The scenery is grand and terrible. I have walked under overhanging rocks, which seemed only to need the pressure of a finger to send them down headlong. Many of them resemble the ruins of

44

old castles, and it needs but a little imagination to fancy yourself in the deserted hall of a temple or palace."

Passing Fort Bridger, the company "crossed over a high mountain so long and steep as to make it very hard on the oxen. We had ten yoke to each wagon. On descending we came to Bear River, a swift stream abounding with trout and thickly bordered with trees. We encamped on its banks."

Finally, on September 26 they had their first view of the Salt Lake Valley. "Here we were met by several men with teams, ready to assist those who needed help. The descent of the mountain was very steep and awfully dangerous for about four miles. . . . When I arrived at the base of the mountain I turned to look at the coming wagons, and was actually terrified to see them rushing down, though both wheels were locked, and no accident occurred."

On September 28, within a few miles of their destination, Jean wrote:

> Of all the splendid scenery and awful roads that have ever been since creation, I think this day's journey has beaten them all. We had encamped last night at the foot of a mountain which we had to ascend this morning. This was hard enough on our poor worn out animals, but the road after was completely covered with stones as large as bushel boxes, stumps of trees, with here and there mudholes in which our poor oxen sunk to the knees. Added to all this there was Kanyon Creek, a stream of water running at the bottom of a deep ravine, which intersected our road in such a zigzag fashion that we had to ford it sixteen times. One of my teams was forced down an incline with such rapidity that one of the oxen fell into the stream and was drowned before it could be extricated. This makes six oxen I have lost in the journey. . . .
>
> The grandeur of the scenery to my mind takes away all fear, and while standing in admiration at the view, Milton's expressions in his "Paradise Lost" came forcibly to my recollection. "These are thy glorious works. Parent of good, in wisdom hast thou made them all." And I seemed to forget all the hardships of our long journey. Suddenly I heard a sound as of rushing waters on my left hand and looking in that direction I observed that the mountain stream buried itself among some bushes and, sure enough, there was the prettiest waterfall I have seen yet. . . . The cataract itself was comprised of fifteen separate falls, over as many pieces of rock; the whole perpendicular height being about thirty-five or

forty feet. It struck me with both awe and delight. I felt as though I would like to have lingered a long time watching it.

At sunset they emerged from the canyon and caught a faint view of the valley that was to be their home. They camped in a hollow just at the entrance of the valley. The next day she wrote: "Rose this morning with a thankful heart that our travels are nearly finished. I can hardly analyze my feelings, but the prevailing ones are joy and gratitude for the protecting care had over me and mine during our long and perilous journey."

Jean and her family spent the first few days in Salt Lake at the home of a Sister Wallace, whose husband, a missionary in England, had sent a letter to his wife with Jean. On October 6 Jean purchased a small four-room house with an acre of garden attached to it. She was especially pleased with the garden, which contained Indian corn, potatoes, cabbages, carrots, parsnips, beets, and tomatoes.

After traveling around the Salt Lake Valley, she went to Ogden, where she purchased twenty acres of land and arranged to have a small house built during the winter. While there she was shown several specimens of produce. "I brought home with me a pumpkin weighing fifty-three pounds, but I saw some weighing ninety pounds, also potatoes weighing three pounds and perfectly sound throughout."

The following March she moved to Ogden with her son William and the younger children. "Now I suppose I have finished my ramblings for my whole life," she mistakenly concluded.

The Ogden experience was not happy. In September 1869 Jean wrote:

I have been 18 years this day an inhabitant of Utah territory, and I may say 18 years of hard toil and continual disappointment. My 20 acre farm turned out to be a mere saleratum patch, killing the seed that was sown instead of producing a crop. After spending 7 years work on it, we abandoned it and I am now living in Ogden City in a small log house, and working at my trade as a dressmaker. The famine of the year '57 and the move South in '58 are matters of history, and I need only say that I passed through both and a bitter experience it was. I have buried my youngest boy at 9 years of age. William has been married 11 years. Edward and

John went to California—Edward in '53 and John in '50. They could not stand poverty any longer so ran away from it. I sometimes think I shall go, too, but I must leave that for the future to decide. . . . I should hate to leave [my daughter] and her brothers, and I have no idea they would like to leave their homes, as they all have young families.

I have tried to do my best in the various circumstances in which I have been placed. I came here in what I believed to be a revelation of the Most High God, trusting in the assurances of the missionaries, whom I believed to have the Spirit of Truth. I left my home, sacrificed my property, broke up every dear association, and what was and is yet, dearer than all, left my beloved native land, and for what? A bubble that has burst in my grasp! It has been a severe lesson, but I can say it has led me to lean more on my Heavenly Father, and less on men's words. In 1864 I married Mr. Edward Pearce. I had been a widow 15 years. . . . I hoped that my old age would have been cheered by his companionship—that I would no longer be alone. But it was not to be—he lived only 6 months, but that was a time of unbroken peace and comfort, and his sudden death was a severe blow to me. Perhaps I was not worthy of being the wife of so good a man, for he certainly was one "in whom there was no guile."

Two months later, Jean visited her sons in San Francisco. They persuaded her to remain with them, although she resolutely insisted on working "at my trade so as not to be burdensome to my children till old age prevents me from helping myself. And then the sons and daughters that God has given me I know will look after my comfort."

In 1875 she visited her children and friends in Utah, returning to California in the spring of 1877. On her seventieth birthday she made this reflective diary entry:

Well may I say "Hitherto has the Lord helped me." I have good health and am spending my time among my children, sometimes at one home, sometimes another. . . . I do not suppose I will have any more entries to make in this journal that will be of any interest. My life bids fair to be a very quiet one. I have every temporal comfort my heart can desire. My children vie with each other in contributing to my happiness, and I can truly say I have but one wish unfulfilled. That is that I may live to see every one of my children and grandchildren faithful members of the Kingdom of God. I can not expect to see many more birthdays and as every hour brings me nearer to the final one, I feel to say with Toplady,

"When I draw this fleeting breath, when my eyelids close in death, when I rise to worlds unknown, and behold Thy Judgement Throne, Rock of Ages, shelter me, let me hide myself in Thee."

Three years later at the age of seventy-three, Jean Baker Pearce passed away, leaving a large Mormon posterity in Utah and California, and in her diary an eloquent record of one immigrant's gathering experience.

2

Settling the West

*T*he Mormon migration west continued for many years after 1846. By wagon, handcart, and eventually railroad, Latter-day Saints continued to gather in the Great Basin. Until the mid-1880s, gathering was an official Church policy.

Even after gathering to Utah, the pioneering was far from over. To be sure, some immediately staked out a claim in the Salt Lake Valley, built a house, and within a year or two were settled for the rest of their lives. But others were called upon to uproot their families and head out for a new location in Utah, Arizona, Idaho, Nevada, California, Wyoming, and eventually Mexico and Canada. The gospel ensign to the nations was intended to wave over North and South America and eventually the world, carried forth from a secure base in the Great Basin. Historian Milton R. Hunter listed 350 settlements established during Brigham Young's lifetime, and each of them was, for its settlers, a new exodus and a new beginning.

The initial gathering place for this period was, of course, Salt Lake City. Among its most prominent leaders was Bishop Edwin D. Woolley, who presided over the Thirteenth Ward for twenty-seven years. A practical man with an independent streak, Bishop Woolley's primary concern was the temporal and spiritual welfare of his people. Occasionally he locked horns with Brigham Young and Eliza R. Snow, but they were able to work through their differences with some judicious give and take.

Charles Walker was a salt-of-the-earth Saint who responded to the colonizing call with a simple faith and an accepting heart, and who endured the deprivations of pioneering with an ebullient sense of humor.

Lucy White Flake was born in the Church, in Illinois. She walked across the plains with her family and helped settle Lehi, Cedar City, and Beaver, Utah, then Allen's Camp and Snowflake, Arizona. Though her husband was not religious when they married, largely through her persistent efforts he eventually became one of the pillars of the Church in Arizona. Lucy's poignant autobiography reveals her heartache at plural marriage, and her alternate fortitude and depression through the hardships of pioneering.

Edward Bunker was a member of the Mormon Battalion and a missionary to England. He led a company of handcart pioneers across the plains, served as a bishop in Ogden and Santa Clara, Utah, and founded Bunkerville, Nevada. His experience with the Santa Clara and Bunkerville United Orders helps us appreciate the difficulties encountered by those who tried to implement the economic ideals inspired by the revelations of Joseph Smith.

Of all the colonizations attempted in the generation after Brigham Young, none was more grueling than settling the San Juan region of southeastern Utah. In fact, it is hard to imagine how any settlement, at any place or time, could have demanded more than this incredible journey down the Hole-in-the-Rock chute as told through the experience of the Lemuel H. Redd family.

Chauncey West's 1895 diary gives us a view of the life and times of an extraordinary young man in Brigham City, Utah.

Chapter 6

Edwin Woolley:
Bishop of the
Thirteenth Ward

Edwin D. Woolley came from a
long line of Pennsylvania Quakers. Born in 1807, he grew up
on a farm in Newlin Township, Pennsylvania, and the Quaker
influence of his early years affected his entire life. In fact, long
after he became a Mormon, Edwin continued to use the deeply
ingrained expressions *thee* and *thou.*

In 1831 Edwin married a young Quaker, Mary Wickersham,
and began a farm of his own. When his father died, Edwin and
Mary shouldered the responsibility for the younger brothers
and sisters. They moved to Ohio in 1832 and purchased a
quarter section of land. In April 1837 Edwin moved his family
half a mile from the farm to East Rochester, Ohio, where he
opened a mercantile business.

In East Rochester, Edwin heard stories about Joseph
Smith, whom some called "the Prophet." One day, two
missionaries, George A. Smith and Lorenzo D. Barnes, visited
the Woolley home, and in November 1837 Mary Woolley was
baptized.

To test her Edwin said, "Mary, I will give thee a new silk
dress if thou wilt say that Joseph is not a Prophet." But Mary
valued her testimony more than a silk dress and remained true
to her convictions.

Intrigued by what he saw and heard, Edwin decided to visit the Prophet himself. He and Mary rode ninety miles to Kirtland on horseback in one day—a strenuous feat—only to find that Joseph had gone to Missouri. However, they did meet the Prophet's father, and persuaded him to spend the winter with them in East Rochester.

Undoubtedly Joseph Smith, Sr., influenced Edwin's decision to be baptized. It was cold and blustery on Christmas Eve, 1837 when Edwin joined the Church. On Christmas day he was ordained a high priest and set apart to preside over the East Rochester branch.

Keenly aware of his inexperience in the Church, Edwin felt inadequate to lead. Once, kneeling in prayer with his wife and family, he began, "Our Father in Heaven," and stopped. Turning to Mary, he asked, "What shall I say next? Thee has been in the Church longer than I have."

In the spring of 1839, upon returning from a mission to Pennsylvania, Edwin finally met the Prophet Joseph in Quincy, Illinois. The main body of the Church had just been driven from Missouri, and Joseph invited Edwin to help select a site in Illinois where the Saints could gather and live in peace.

The site chosen was Commerce, which Joseph renamed Nauvoo. The Woolleys moved there in 1840 and opened a general store. One day, the Prophet walked in, surveyed the well-stocked shelves, and said, "Brother Woolley, we want all your goods for the building up of the Kingdom of God." After Joseph left, Edwin boxed up all his goods except those previously committed to Saint Louis companies. When the Prophet returned, Edwin asked if he should deliver the goods somewhere or if the Prophet would call for them. Joseph, deeply moved, told him to return the goods to the shelves and go on with his business. Edwin had passed the test.

Edwin's loyalty to the Prophet and his devotion to the cause involved him in many important events in early Church history. The revelation on plural marriage was read for the first time in Edwin's home in October 1843. He accepted it as a revelation from God and became one of the first to comply with it, marrying Louisa Gordon and Ellen Wilding. Louisa was a convert from New York who had been previously married; and Ellen, a servant in the Woolley home, had been converted in England by Heber C. Kimball.

Mary consented to Edwin's plural marriages but found it difficult to live with the tensions of plurality and returned to her parents' home in East Rochester. After a short time, however, she became converted to the principle and rejoined Edwin in Nauvoo.

On the day Joseph and Hyrum left for Carthage Jail in 1844, they stopped at the Woolley home. There, according to Edwin, Joseph uttered the famous words, "I am going like a lamb to the slaughter; but I am calm as a summer's morning."

After the expulsion from Nauvoo in 1846, the fifteen Woolleys—Edwin, Mary, Louisa, Ellen, their seven children, and four relatives—spent the winter on the banks of the Missouri at Winter Quarters. At Brigham Young's request, Edwin remained in Winter Quarters for another year to operate the store which outfitted the Saints for their trek to the Rocky Mountains.

Finally, on 27 May 1848 Edwin and his family left Winter Quarters for the Salt Lake Valley. Louisa chose to remain behind and died the following year. Mary accompanied Edwin and five weeks later, on July 5, she gave birth to a baby girl, Mary Louisa, at Goose Creek, Nebraska, on the north bank of the Platte River. Mary Louisa was to become the mother of J. Reuben Clark, Jr.

The Woolleys entered the Salt Lake Valley in September 1848 and camped outside the Old Fort. When lots were assigned, Edwin received a lot on the corner of what is now Third East and Third South streets. He built an adobe house which was so small that part of the family had to live in the wagon beds just outside the door of the house. He was also allotted a tract of land south of the city and began farming.

On 12 February 1849 Edwin became a member of the high council of the first stake in the Great Salt Lake Valley, a position he held for ten years, including the first five years he served as bishop of the Thirteenth Ward.

In 1849 Brigham called Edwin to go east to assist with

emigration and purchase of supplies for the Church. In Saint Louis he met a young English convert, Mary Ann Olpin, whom he engaged to care for his son and to cook for the company on the return trip. In the fall of 1850, Mary Ann became the fourth Mrs. Woolley.

Edwin farmed, operated a mercantile establishment, and managed Brigham Young's personal business affairs for several years. In September 1851 he was elected to the Utah House of Representatives. He was an incorporator of the Deseret Telegraph Company and of Zion's Cooperative Mercantile Institution, and served several terms as Salt Lake County Recorder.

In 1854 Edwin was called to serve as bishop of the Thirteenth Ward. When he said he needed some time to decide whom to call as his counselors, Brigham Young replied that until they were selected, he, President Young, and Heber C. Kimball would serve as counselors. Edwin quickly named Briant Stringham and John W. Woolley, his son.

The responsibilities of a bishop during the latter half of the nineteenth century were enormous. Bishop Woolley saw that the ward was fenced in to protect the gardens and orchards from stray livestock; that a ward school was built and staffed; that ward dances, musicals, and theatricals were properly supervised; that his ward's quota of laborers fulfilled their public works assignments; that ward members were instructed in improved methods of agriculture and livestock breeding; and that the members of his ward behaved like Saints. In short, he was the ward's business and domestic affairs advisor as well as its pastor.

For all practical purposes, the Latter-day Saints living between Main Street and Third East, and South Temple and Third South belonged to the Thirteenth Ward Church. Every church activity was organized, directed, and carried out in the ward. Bishop Woolley introduced and directed programs, collected tithes and contributions, and relayed doctrinal pronouncements and policy decisions. He solicited volunteers for colonizing and preaching missions and arranged for teamsters to transport immigrants from the east.

As "a judge in Israel," he was the mediator, arbitrator, and conciliator in all disputes. Any difficulties between ward members which could not be settled privately—and there were many—were settled by the bishop. He was the representative of the members in his ward in dealing with Church, city, and territorial officials. He was, in short, their advocate, defender, planner, and foreman.

With these enormous responsibilities, Edwin Woolley's success and longevity as bishop of the Thirteenth Ward for twenty-seven years was remarkable.

Bishop Woolley insisted on running a tight ship. In his first talk at the biweekly bishops' meeting, he said, "A bishop should act as a father to the people, who should be obedient to him as children to their parents. And the bishop should not require of the people what they are unable to do, so that his reasonable requests may be respected and attended to."

He relied heavily on the Aaronic Priesthood of his ward. They were the legs and feet of the bishop, as he put it. The offices of deacon, teacher, and priest were by no means limited to young men; in fact, the large majority of Aaronic Priesthood holders were adults. Priesthood appointments were not determined by age, but by suitability for the task. Deacons helped the bishop with meetinghouse maintenance and harvested the crops of elders and seventies away on missions. Elders, seventies, and high priests functioned as members of the deacons quorum while performing these tasks.

Teachers were appointed to visit families, report their spiritual and temporal condition to the bishop, and help provide for their needs. For example, they helped immigrants take out citizenship papers, raised money for the Perpetual Emigration Fund and public works projects, and encouraged ward members to unity and obedience in the gospel. Generally, "teachers" held the Melchizedek Priesthood and were "on loan," so to speak, to the bishop and the teachers quorum.

Priests officiated in administering the sacrament, conducted baptismal services, preached, and in some instances served as branch presidents.

Bishop Woolley had a gift for pastoral care. He was

concerned with the practical application of the gospel in the lives of ordinary people. Not particularly inclined to theology, he declared that he "did not like so much extra faith, but liked to see the works."

The Poor Account of the Thirteenth Ward's ledger books demonstrates Bishop Woolley's concern for the unfortunate: donations to a woman with cancer, donations toward building a house for a poor family, and appropriations for the "poor hands" working on the temple. Under Bishop Woolley's direction, the teachers collected all kinds of things for the needy—tea, soap, matches, candles, sugar, coffee, eggs, butter, cheese, apples, rice, clothing, burial shrouds, and children's books.

Edwin Woolley cared for his people and worked unstintingly for their welfare. He was an effective bishop not only because he worked hard but because he was not afraid to take responsibility in his calling. Contrary to the anti-Mormon stereotypes of the nineteenth century, Brigham Young's bishops were not sycophants or lackeys. When they disagreed, he did not call for their resignations but respected them for their exercise of judgment and their right to inspiration. At times, Bishop Woolley demonstrated his independent spirit by resisting new programs and methods. When the Sunday Schools were organized, for example, he waited several years to see how they would function before implementing the program. When ward Relief Societies were instituted in 1867 and 1868, the Thirteenth Ward was one of the last to comply. Bishop Woolley explained, "It is not my habit to be in a hurry in our movements, nor do I wish the Sisters to rush in their movements, but be cool and deliberate. . . . In time we will be ahead of those who have moved so fast." Bishop Woolley wanted to be certain the new organization functioned under him, not alongside or above him. At the organizational meeting of his ward's Relief Society, he emphasized, "I wish to select such sisters for officers as will listen to my counsel, and to carry out such measures as I shall suggest from time to time."

Nor did Bishop Woolley hesitate to counsel against some of the programs proposed by Eliza R. Snow, president of the general Relief Society. For example, when Sister Snow urged the sisters to plant mulberry trees and begin a silk culture, he expressed doubt that the project would succeed, and told his ward Relief Society to drag their feet on it.

When Brigham Young held a Church-wide price convention in 1864 to establish uniform prices, Bishop Woolley resisted. "We may understand some general things alike," he said, "but the minutia we cannot all understand until they transpire. The time has not yet come when all can see eye to eye. If we wait patiently we will see things come out all right."

Bishop Woolley demonstrated his tolerance for dissent by aiding his heretical counselor (1864-1869) William S. Godbe. Godbe had been out of harmony with Church policies for some time before he organized a spiritualist movement called the Church of Zion. During the months that followed that tragic schism, Bishop Woolley permitted the leaders of the Godbeite movement to hold meetings in the Thirteenth Ward assembly rooms. Knowing that Godbe had been a respected counselor, Bishop Woolley deemed it prudent to "answer" the dissidents after each of their Sunday meetings. The Godbeites responded the following week. Thus, a series of debates on the New Movement, as it was called, was held in the ward meetinghouse.

Bishop Woolley survived this period with only one important tiff with Brigham Young, in February 1870. The issue was not the rental of the Thirteenth Ward hall to the Godbeites, but its rental for a dance. Bishop Woolley had hoped the dance would help raise money to refurbish the building; but when President Young learned the ward would be competing with the Church's Social Hall, he reprimanded the bishop in the School of the Prophets. The ward meetinghouse, he said, should be used only for "sacred purposes." After all, that was why they had built the Salt Lake Theatre and Social Hall.

The bishop contritely replied that he never would have rented the hall if he had known the authorities were opposed to it. He explained the ward's financial condition. The people wanted a place "for fun and frolic," but were unable to raise the funds needed to repair the building. There were some persons who owned thousands of dollars of property in the ward, he said, but they were so stingy they would not give five dollars without a half hour's sermon on consecration.

Brigham Young's counselor George A. Smith commented that while he recognized there were problems in restricting social events to the Social Hall, he was opposed as a matter of policy to using ward meetinghouses for theatrical plays and dances. Bishop Woolley chuckled and whispered to a friend nearby, "You see, President Smith is coming over to my side."

At the opening of the School of the Prophets the following week, President Young called on Bishop Woolley to say whether he did not mean *him* when he said there were some who owned thousands of dollars of property in the ward yet would require a half hour's preaching before they would make a five dollar contribution. Bishop Woolley denied that he had President Young in mind.

Then the President asked whether the bishop did not build the assembly rooms of the ward for the express purpose of competing with the Social Hall. No, Bishop Woolley replied, though he thought the rental for the Social Hall was "too high in price" and the hall too small in size. President Young defended the fee and asked whether it was true that he had said that President George A. Smith was coming over to his (Bishop Woolley's) side on the issue. George Q. Cannon and Joseph F. Smith arose to confirm that they had distinctly overheard the bishop make the statement. Bishop Woolley looked a little chagrined. President George A. Smith then arose and said that inasmuch as "he was believed to be going over to Bishop Woolley's side, he would now make a motion that Bishop Woolley take a mission to Europe."

Immediately, Edwin jumped up and expressed deep regret for having hurt the feelings of his brethren. He asked for forgiveness and pleaded, "Brethren, please don't send me on a mission to Europe to atone for what I have done. If I deserve to be punished, let it be done here."

Having made his point, President Young was magnanimous: "I do not remember ever having sent a man on a mission to punish him," he declared. "We send men on missions to do them good—to give them a chance to get the spirit of God." President Smith then substituted another motion, which was carried, that Bishop Woolley "be allowed a further trial as a bishop." Bishop Woolley continued that "further trial" until his death eleven years later.

Woolley family members today who admire the contrariness of their progenitor enjoy the story that once Brigham Young said that if Bishop Woolley should fall off his horse while crossing to the other side of the Jordan, they should not look for him floating downstream. Instead, they would find him swimming upstream, obstinately contending against the current.

On one occasion, according to the family, the bishop and Brigham had a heated discussion about a business deal. President Young, who could be very sarcastic, turned as he was leaving and said, "Now, Bishop Woolley, I guess you will go off and apostatize." To which Edwin rejoined, "If this were your church, President Young, I would be tempted to do so. But this is just as much my church as it is yours, and why should I apostatize from my own church?"

Despite their disagreements, Brigham Young dearly loved his outspoken bishop. In a painting commissioned by Brigham Young called "President Young and His Friends," Bishop Woolley is depicted along with Heber C. Kimball, Daniel H. Wells, George A. Smith, and four others.

Beginning in the middle 1850s, Edwin and his brother Samuel Amos Woolley operated a store in the Deseret or Tithing Store Building located on the present site of the Hotel Utah, just east of Temple Square. As he prospered, Bishop Woolley commissioned Truman O. Angell, architect of the Salt Lake Temple, to build a home for him on the corner of State Street and Social Hall Avenue. It was one of the finest houses west of the Missouri River. In this home Edwin's first wife Mary died in 1859, after a long illness. Edwin wrote a long letter to her nonmember family in Ohio: "I do not know, but some of you may think that [as] I have other wives and children, that my first wife may have been neglected, but for your comfort in this trying hour I will say to you, she was my first wife, the wife of my youth and for whom I never lost my first love. She is as dear today to me as the day I took her from your door and never has it been otherwise."

When Bishop Woolley died in 1881 at the age of seventy-four, he left 334 living descendants, the basis for a large, prominent family. Among his descendants are J. Reuben Clark, Jr., and Spencer Woolley Kimball.

The *Deseret News* obituary made this apt characterization: "Bishop Edwin D. Woolley was a good and useful man. It is doubtful if one more industrious could be found anywhere. His life was one continuing scene of endeavor. He was exceedingly outspoken, uttering his sentiments sometimes without much regard to consequences. . . . Under his unusual frankness of speech, he carried a kind and manly heart."

Chapter 7

Charles L. Walker: Sage of Saint George

It was Sunday, 19 August 1862—
a pleasant day, Charley Walker noted. He and his wife Abigail
were listening to the Brethren in the Bowery on Temple
Square. "Bro D Spencer and HC Kimball gave us some good
exhortations pertaining to our duties. At the close of the
meeting 250 men were called to go to the Cotton Country. My
name is on the List."

Cotton country. That meant Saint George. A year before,
Brigham Young had called several hundred Saints to southern
Utah—Dixie—to raise the crop most in demand since the War
Between the States began. Now, only a year later, the success of
the cotton mission was far from certain.

Charley had emigrated from England to build the kingdom
and there would be no turning back. Still, moving again was
not easy. "Here I have worked for the last 7 years thro heat and
cold, hunger and adverse circumstances, and at last have got
me a home, a Lot with fruit trees just beginning to bear and
look pretty. Well, I must leave it and go and do the will of My
Father in Heaven who over rules all for the good of them that
love and fear him, and I pray God to give me Strength to
accomplish that which is required of me in an acceptable
manner before him."

Saint George was dry and forbidding. When he arrived, Charley observed, "St. George is a barren looking place. . . . Very windy, dusty, blowing nearly all the time. The water is not good and far from being palatable. And this is the country we have to live in and make it blossom as the Rose. Well its all right; we shall know how to appreciate a good country when we get to it, when the Lord has prepared the way for his People to return and build up the waste places of Zion."

Charley was allocated a city lot and a two-and-a-half acre garden plot, but his farming experience was minimal. In Salt Lake City he had worked as a blacksmith. His peach trees had succeeded, though, so he planted seventy-five in Saint George. Unfortunately the water supply was meager, and the crops for the first season were "light, very light, in fact I might say a failure." All but six of Charley's peach trees died. He supported himself and Abigail, and daughter Zaidee by blacksmithing, gardening, and doing various odd jobs. Later he worked as a stonemason on the Saint George Tabernacle and Temple, and served as assistant marshal and as lieutenant in the local militia.

As for the Church assignments, Charley, who had served as the president of the Saint Louis teachers quorum in 1854, was appointed "Seventies Teacher" in 1863, arbitrating disputes between seventies and enjoining faithful obedience to the commandments; and in 1869 he was called to the bishopric of the Saint George First Ward.

In 1864 Charley received the disappointing news that his father and stepmother had left Salt Lake City and returned to the States. "Alas poor man," Charley reflected,

left the Kingdom of God after being in for many years, and now has left the only place of Safety. Strange how blind men will get. In my experience when a man or Woman raise ther heel against the Lord's annointed, tenfold darknes shrouds them. Then the Devil binds them with his chains and leads them wither so ever he will. A man may lack money, Bread, friends, and the nessesary comforts of life; he may be hunted and persecuted and driven by ruthles mobs; his Family may turn against him; his bosom friends may betray him. All these he may suffer and get rewarded for, but when he loses the Holy Ghost he is then in hell and his

concience continualy upbraids him of once having had the light
of the Holy Spirit but through Sin and transgression has lost it
with no hope of ever receiving it again in this world or the next.
Oh, how child like a saint ought to live, to secure Salvation and
Eternal Life.

Charley was soon to learn what it was to lack both money
and bread, for the drought of 1864 destroyed the crops and
many went hungry. But he retained his inherent optimism and
good humor. In 1867 he composed new lyrics for "Marching
through Georgia," recounting the struggles of pioneering
Saint George. One of the seven stanzas goes:

Some six or seven years ago this country looked forlorn,
A God-forsaken country, as sure as you are born.
The lizards crept around it, and thorns immense had grown,
As we came marching to Dixie.

Chorus

Hurrah! Hurrah! The thorns we have cut down.
Hurrah! Hurrah. We're building quite a town.
St. George is growing greater, and gaining great renown,
Since we came marching to Dixie.

We've battled with the mineral, we've battled with our foes,
We've battled with the Virgin, that everybody knows;
Our deseret homes are pretty and blossom like the rose,
Since we came marching to Dixie.

Charley was a popular toastmaster, poet, and singer. He
played in the brass band which played on festive occasions, and
marched with the militia. ("Went to the regimental drill on the
public square. Quite a bungling time of it. Played twice with
the Band, and sang the 'Loafers-lament.' ")

For the young people's literary club he wrote poems,
composed and sang songs, lectured, acted, and debated. (A
typical debate topic was, "What has done more for the benefit
of mankind, the honeybee or the silk worm?")

The club members decided to publish a newspaper, but
they didn't have a printing press. So they took a large sheet of

paper about legal size and folded it in half, producing a four-page folio. Across the top they wrote the title *Veprecula* (Latin for "little bramble bush"). The titled but otherwise blank "newspaper" was handed to one of the members of the club, who became responsible to fill in the first column. He or she wrote a little essay, joke, or story, and handed it to the next person, and so on until the sheet was completely filled. Then another sheet was folded, titled, dated and started on its way.

Charley, who used the pen name "Mark Whiz," almost always came up with something lighthearted. For example, his recipe for Dixie soup:

> As provisions are scarce and hard to obtain, we thought it would not be amiss to give our readers the following items to make a good soup. Take a pair of old stoga boots. Carefully skin them and take out the kidney tallow. Cut them into sizable pieces. Put them into a large iron pot with ten gallons of rain water. As soon as the water is warm, add three quarts of the best show pegs you can buy. Also 10 1/2 oz. of Hungarian tacks and a pound of brass buttons. Let it simmer for 2 hours, then add a trace of colts revolvers and a quantity of stone cutters mallets for dumplings. Let it boil for 1 hour. Stir in 5 oz. of indigo for seasoning. To be served in canteens with 10 penny nails for spoons. To be eaten while hot with nicely browned pieces of an old red flannel shirt.

Through times of hardship and deprivation Charley's good-natured humor buoyed the Saints. "Oh poverty!" he once wrote, "thou poor man's companion. How close thou dost stick! If thou wouldst leave me and visit some opulent scamp my tears would be few at our parting."

But Charley Walker contributed more than humor. When construction of the Saint George Tabernacle began, Charley was among the first workers. In 1872 he wrote, "I have worked on this building for over 5 year[s], from putting in the Foundation to the capstone on the tower. Many weary toilsome days have I labored on the St. George Tabernacle, lifting the heavy rocks in the wind, dust, cold, and scorching heat of this climate, yet I have felt happy and contented. I was called to labor there by the Priesthood, letting my own affairs go, to work on those walls, yet through the hard times of scarcity and want of the necessaries of life I have been blessed."

66

Along with the blessings, however, also came trials. As Charley noted in 1866, "It seems there is always something to mar our little portion of happiness while sojourning here below. It is some consolation to know it will not last forever." Occasionally even Charley Walker's light heart became weighed down. One day "I felt as though I was alone and not a friend in the world above or below. Felt as solemn as tho I was passing thro the House of Death."

Unfortunately, death was not a stranger to most pioneer families, and Charley's was no exception. He lost four infants or young children to sickness, and two married daughters. On the death of his little Mary, Charley wrote,

> I got home and saw the little thing in agony and great pain, its little hands clinched and writhing in convulsions. I took her on my lap, and in about an hour She breathed her last. I placed her in her Mother's lap and said, here take your Baby; She's dead. Then their was a shriek and wail that seemed to go thro me and chill my heart's blood. Oh, God, how can I stand to have the little cherub torn from me by the hand of Death. . . . I sat up all night alone with the corpse. How quiet and solemn the hours passed away and as the grey twilight appeared I looke[d] forth with dread at that which was yet to come: the singing and other funeral ceremonies and the laying of the dear one away in its cold and narrow bed in the graveyard.

At the funeral service Charley "could not hear or understand much as my thoughts were on the contents of the little black coffin before me, and it seemed to me as tho I shou[l]d choke with grief. There was 9 wagons conveyed the People to the grave. Br Peirce offered up the dedecatory prayer, and the dirt soon hid from our sight our little angel Mary."

Charley was not one to dwell long on tragedy. His native character was resilient and inclined him to be grateful for blessings rather than to lament his losses. He enjoyed life, especially the camaraderie of the Saints. On 14 June 1867 he described a local celebration. "Hot. With quite a goodly number of citizens I went 9 miles up the Santa Clara River and spent the day in recreation: eating, drinking, singing, swinging, dancing, romping, and shouting. In short, casting off all but to make merry. A good feeling prevaild. No intoxicating drinks were used. No tabacco smoking (and a very little chewing). All were happy, sober, lighthearted, enjoying themsleves as Saints only can."

From time to time Charley visited Salt Lake City to attend conference and see old friends. Returning to Saint George on one occasion he reflected, "This place when contrasted with the bustle and business of Salt Lake, seems very dull. A person can walk upon this town for hours and scarce see a man—no business, nor railroad nor locomotive whistle nor express wagon, no auctions nor saloon music, no theatres or circus or dances. All still and peace. In fact it seems more like the city of the dead than the living."

If Saint George seemed like a "city of the dead," it was not because there was nothing to do. It was because there was so much to do—so much work on the farms that the town seemed deserted. Somewhat apologetically Charley attributed the lapses in his journal to routine work: "Sometimes I don't think it worthy of note to put down every day when it is the same thing every day over again, work, work, work, eat, sleep, work again, and not much time for mental improvement."

In the spring of 1874 the United Order was organized in Saint George. Charley and the other Saints were rebaptized prior to entering the order: "Having Authority given me of Jesus Christ, I baptize you for the remission of your Sins, for the renewal of your covenants, and for the Observance of the Rules of the Holy United Order in the name of the Father, Son and Holy Ghost. Amen." Confirmation followed.

One of the most anxiously awaited events each year was the arrival of Brigham Young and company, for with the president came the advent of the most entertaining and spiritually uplifting season of the year. In 1876 Brigham's party arrived on November 9:

> At work on the Temple. At 2 o clock P.M. the workmen on the Temple marched up to the Court House in their working clothes two abreast to welcome Pres Young and Party. We had two Banners: on one was Holliness to the Lord, the all seeing eye; and

68

Zion's workmen on the other, which I carried. At the head of the column was "Welcome to Brigham Young our chief Builder." We all formed in single line on the northside of the Road and as the Pres and Party passed, we took off our hats and bowed to them. They returned the salute. We then marched in the same order down to the Temple and resumed the work.

On another occasion Charley had an encounter with Brigham that he treasured all his life. He had written a special temple anthem, which Brigham heard in church. After the meeting, he asked for a copy and Charley

went home and got the song and took it to him. He treated me very kindly and asked me to sit beside him and take dinner with him. I spent the time very pleasantly and found him to be very polite, genial, and sociable, and I felt quite at home in Chatting over the work on the Temple, old times and other general topics. In bidding him goodbye He took my hand in both of his and said, God bless you Br Charley, and God has blessed you, hasnt He? It seemed that in an instant all the blessings I ever received were before Me. My emotion was too much to answer him and I chokingly said, I have learned to trust in the Lord.

On 1 January 1877 Brigham Young presided at the dedication of the Saint George Temple. After Wilford Woodruff read the dedicatory prayer on the main floor, the choir and congregation sang Charley's "Temple Dedication Song." Then the ailing Brigham Young was carried upstairs and the Saints reassembled for the dedication of the second floor and sealing room.

Eight days later Charley stood at the baptismal font to witness the first baptism in the new temple. Brigham's daughter Susa Young Dunford (Gates) was baptized for a deceased friend, and Charley "could not refrain from shedding tears of joy on beholding the commencement of so great a work in the Temple of our God. Hossanna [to] God and the Lamb."

On January 12 Charley was married in the temple to Sarah Smith. "Glory to God in the highest," wrote Charley. "In spite of tradition my wife [Abigail] acted a noble part . . . and showed her true womanhood. God bless her and preserve her in the truth forever." Eventually, Abagail and Sarah each gave birth to eight children.

Before leaving Saint George in the spring, Brigham Young organized a stake, and soon Charley was released from his position in the bishopric. "The Authorities here have appointed a Bishop and two councillors for each ward. . . . This relieves me of being a Bishop's second councillor and presiding teacher in the ward in which I have acted for nearly 7 years. I feel it is all right that the change should be made . . . yet I always felt a pleasure in performing the duties, and [for] those that can do more good than me, I am willing to step aside that good may be accomplished."

When word of Brigham Young's death on 29 August 1877 reached St. George, stores and businesses closed and the Saints mourned. The next night a special meeting was held in the Saint George Temple. Afterward, Charley Walker remained alone in the temple as the night guard. Sitting there in the quiet, in the darkness of the night, he reflected on the death of his beloved president. "Felt calm and very solemn," he wrote. "Well do I remember his words to me just before he left St George. 'Well good-bye Brother Charley Walker, God bless you and may peace be Multiplied upon you.' And now he sleeps. The greatest, best and most noble man of the age. Peace to his ashes and praise to his memory."

Following the death of Brigham Young, the federal government increased its pressure on Latter-day Saints practicing plural marriage. The Supreme Court ruled the religious freedom clause of the Constitution was not a justifiable defense. The Court's decision irked Charley, who wrote a poem expressing his feelings (as well, no doubt, the feelings of many other Saints):

An Address to the American Eagle

Illustrious Bird! Majestic Fowl!
Are you deaf?
Can't you hear the nations howl,
Their sighs of grief?
I thought your pinions broad and strong—
Can't you hear?
Would shield the right, redress the wrong:
Ah—a tear.

70

And why that tear, most noble bird?
Ain't you well?
Or is it what we've lately heard
Sounds like hell?
Illustrious Bird in doleful plight,
Can't you cluck?
Or are you meditating flight?
Say are you stuck?
Your crest seems fallen, your plumage soiled.
What—no reply?
What is the matter? are you riled?
What? going to cry?
. . . .

The sickly bird said, "Pray, don't joke.
I don't feel well.
My Constitution's nearly broke.
Can't break the spell."
. . . .

The Noble Bird raised high his beak
And left them in the lurch
And made his home on Utah's peak
And since has joined the Church.

In 1892 Charley was arrested and fined six cents for unlawful cohabitation (the customary charge made by the government against polygamists). Through the rest of his years he continued to write poems and songs and kept up his journal. Year after year he expected the call to return to Jackson County, Missouri. It never came, but he never lost faith.

A few newspapers published some of Charley's essays and poems, and half a dozen of his hymns were included, at one time, in the Latter-day Saint hymnbook. But until his death in 1904, Charley Walker was mostly known to and loved by the pioneers of Utah's "Dixie."

Chapter 8

Lucy White Flake:
Pioneering
Utah and Arizona

Lucy Hannah White was born in 1842 in Knox County, Illinois, the oldest of Samuel and Mary Burton White's eight children. Her grandparents and parents had joined the Church in England and emigrated to the United States to be with the Saints. Lucy was baptized in the ice-covered Missouri River when she was seven years old and walked across the plains with her family when she was eight.

Shortly after their arrival in Utah, the Whites, including Grandfather White and Lucy's uncles Dennis, Joel, and David, were called to settle a new community thirty-five miles south of Salt Lake City. In her 1894 autobiography, Lucy recalled that they "camped at a butifull spring one mile from the Jordan River. That place is now called Lehi. We spent the winter there, built log houses in the shape of a fort." In the spring a town was surveyed and permanent homes were built. "My Father built two log rooms a little distance apart and afterwards closed it in and made another room. We felt thankfull and happy in our new home. We did not have much to eat, but we always had bread." Lucy's mother, who had been a schoolteacher, "taught me my letters out of the Bible as [we] had not school book."

Lucy was ten when she was rebaptized and confirmed a member of The Church of Jesus Christ of Latter-day Saints in 1852. Her father, a counselor in the bishopric, always attended general conference, but returned somewhat shaken after the October 1852 conference, "and told Mother he was called to move south three Hundred miles. Mother felt dredful bad for she had been seperated from her people so much and now we were setled so near them she thought it was cruel she had to go away so far." Mary gave birth to a son on October 14, and on November 7 the family loaded their possessions into wagons and "started to go where we were called Ceder City Iron County. Uncel Joel White and Uncle David Savage [and] Grandma White went also. We were three weeks on the Road and very cold wether."

The Whites were part of a large group of settlers sent south in 1852 to reinforce Cedar City and Parowan, where the danger of an Indian uprising had increased. Lucy found nearly all the residents of Cedar were "from the old World" and "were so differant from what we were used to when they talked to us we could not understand half [of what] they said. Oh! I was home sick, but we were called and had to make the best of it."

Samuel White purchased a farm and built another house. Lucy attended school in a log cabin which "had no floor or window. Logs with holes boared in and legs put in was our seets." Her father raised sheep, and Lucy learned to spin yarn.

In 1857 the Reformation arrived in southern Utah. "We were called on to repent from all our sins. If we had stole or injured any body we had to make it right. Then we were cathicised [catechized] then rebaptised for our sins. I was then fourteen. Was baptised in February. The chunks of ice was running in the Mill race where we was baptised. These were very inthuseastick times. Many confessions were made."

Five months later word reached Utah that President James Buchanan had ordered federal troops to Utah to put down an alleged "Mormon rebellion." Brigham Young ordered the missionaries home and directed the abandonment of several outlying settlements. Lucy's father and Uncle Joel were sent to help bring the Saints from San Bernardino, California, back to

Utah. When they returned, they brought word of "a good stedy young man" named William Jordan Flake. "While all the others were so Wild and rude, they had much to say of this young mans good qualities and good behavyour. I said I want to see this young man when he comes." Two weeks later Lucy got her wish. William arrived driving a herd of stray horses up from San Bernardino. Uncle Joel invited him and several others home for the evening. Lucy noted, "We all liked his aperance very much."

Tall and well-built, William Jordan Flake was nineteen years old. His parents had joined the Church in Mississippi, moved to Nauvoo, and in 1848 arrived in the Great Basin. In 1851 the Flake family helped settle San Bernardino under the direction of Elders Amasa M. Lyman and Charles C. Rich. William's father was killed when he was thrown from a mule, and his mother died of consumption in January 1855. Elder Lyman looked after William, his brother, and his sister.

On 30 December 1858 William and Lucy were married by Elder Lyman and moved in with part of his family. When the Lymans moved fifty miles north to Beaver three weeks later, William and Lucy went with them. In the spring Lucy's parents also moved to Beaver. William freighted for Elder Lyman and was gone much of the time, so Lucy lived with her parents until October 1859, when the young couple bought a log house and "went to Houskeeping." Their first child, James Madison Flake, was born the next month. "We had verry little to keep house with but we were just as happy as could be. We loved each other and loved our home and felt truely thankfull."

Their marriage was close and affectionate, but Lucy was troubled about their religious differences. "William was not religous, being brought up in California after he was twelve and haveing no father to teach him," she wrote. "This was some what of a trial to me but I loved him and prayed for him in secret." Whenever the teachers spoke to William, "he would say he was going to be religious when he got old."

In January 1861 another son was born, but William and Lucy's joy turned to grief as they watched their sick baby suffer. Day after day he grew weaker and weaker. "It seemed like my

74

prairs did no good but still I kept trying to get my Hevenly Father to here me. Kept Praying but it seemed he could not here me." Finally, on March 20 little William died. "His death was the first trial of my faith. It seemed my prairs had always been answered before."

Nevertheless, Lucy continued to pray and pleaded with William to join her. But praying did not come naturally to him, nor did he share Lucy's desire to be sealed in the Endowment House. In July William left on a three-month freighting trip west. In October Lucy attended general conference with her parents. William arrived during their stay in Salt Lake City. Lucy was very happy to see him and overjoyed when he reported, somewhat dismayed, that their bishop had invited them to go to the Endowment House. "He was so surprised he knew not what to say. If the Bishop had told him he wanted him to go to England he could not [have] felt more surprised. He tried to get excused. Said he did not think himself worthy, but the Bishop would not let him off so he came and told me. I thanked my Hevenly Father. Knew it was in answer to prair. That night I was so thankfull I hardly slept. The 9th October 1861 we received that great blessing and was seled for time and all Eternity." Lucy returned to Beaver with her parents, and William to his freighting. She did not see him for almost three months, until Christmas day.

The Church frequently called on William to freight goods to Utah from California and immigrants from the East. In December 1862 Lucy pleaded with him to pray before he left on his next trip. He promised he would when he got home. Lucy remembered the promise through the winter, and when he returned in March, "he knelt down and praid his first prair I ever herd him pray and I was thankfull and happy to know he was trying to do his duty a little better."

Of the decision to enter plural marriage in 1868, Lucy wrote little—simply, "William concluded to take another Wife. I was quite willing." But Lucy's daughter Roberta recalled it in more detail, the way she must have heard her mother tell it many times. One night, after complimenting her cooking, William sat down with Lucy, took her face in his hands, and asked,

"Lucy dear, could you share your husband with another woman?" I thought at first he was joking, and laughingly answered sure, if I could still retain first place in his affections. He bent his head over until his lips met mine. Each kiss carried the same thrill the first one had. He stood up, and pulled me to him and I noticed a seriousness about him that I had never seen before, as he said, "Lucy I have been counselled to take another wife, if you are willing." I could not speak, nor could I keep the tears out of my eyes. "Don't try to answer me now," he said in his gentlest voice. "I think I know how you feel. I have been struggling with myself for a week, trying to bring myself to ask you this. Think it over, pray over it as I have and then let me know."

Lucy struggled for several days. She poured out her heart in prayer. She went to her mother—who gently refused to advise her. When William returned from his next trip, they put their five children to bed and took a moonlight walk. They sat down on a log and William put his arm around her. Then she asked,

"Will, who is the young lady we are going to marry?" I felt his strong frame quiver, his arm tighten about my waist, heard the catch in his voice as he gasped, "WE?"

"Yes, we." I answered in a voice I hardly recognized, so full was it of unselfishness and self-mastery. "We, of course," I went on. "We were made one a long time ago, you and I,—who are we going to marry?" I asked again.

"Are you sure it is the right thing for us to do?" asked William in a trembling voice, and then I loved him as I never had before because I knew that he had been true to me. Then he told me his struggle had been as hard as mine. If he did not believe the principle was from God, he would never have considered it, but as there was no compulsion to entering into it, he had battled with himself to see if he were good enough to undertake it. I told him no one was more worthy, no one could make a better husband.

Lucy spoke of the fine points of William's future bride, eighteen-year-old Prudence Kartchner, and then cried herself to sleep. Eventually, she was able to console herself with the thought "I had had ten years of blessed association with my man. That could never be taken from me. I was his first, and for ten years, his only love. If in that time I had not found a place in

76

his heart and life that no other could fill—then I had failed."

In her own reminiscence, Lucy recorded the events surrounding the October 1868 marriage. "Sister E[liza] R. Snow asked me was I willing. Said yes. She asked do you think you can live in that principal. I said am quite willing to try. My Mother and sister live in it and I think [I] can do as I was willing and she said Sister you shall never get old and she gave me a great blessing and ever[y] time she saw me that day she blest me."

In the spring of 1874, William and Lucy "went in the United Order. Put in all our property. William was asined the stable to take care of." But in the fall he was called to work on the Saint George Temple. Lucy became seriously ill, and after several requests William returned to Beaver. When the United Order disbanded in 1876, William "gave up the stable . . . [and] commenced to work on his farm." By the spring of 1877, "We had a fine large house. We had geese, ducks, hogs, chickens, horses, and cows. We thought we was fixed for life."

Then William went to the dedication of the Saint George Temple where he was called on a colonizing mission to Arizona. He had been a member of the 1873 expedition that had been unable to locate a suitable site for settlement in Arizona, so the prospect of leaving their comfortable home in Beaver for that desolate region was not appealing. "They gave us six months to get redy to go. . . . The thought of leaving my poor Widowed Mother . . . was cruel it seemed to me and William said he had rather go to England. He felt dredful bad but we was called and there was no other way."

In August Roberta was born. In October William rebaptized his family "as we wished to go and work in the Temple and it was council for all to get baptised before going. . . . I was adopted to my Father and Mother. . . . This labor was a great comfort to us. . . . We recieved our second Washings and anointing. They said as we were coming a way so far we could recieve them but they never had given them to any one so young. . . . We were in Heven sure when we were working in that Holy place but when we get out Satan dubles his forse on a person trying to make up for the good one recieves."

Returning to Beaver, William and Lucy sold their farm and in October 1877 loaded their eight children and belongings into five wagons drawn by nine yoke of oxen and seven span of horses. They also drove two hundred head of cattle and forty horses with them.

The weather "was dredful cold, colder than it had been. . . . Prudence had three very bad spells of sickeness. We had five men besides our familey to do for. Most all the work fell to me. I stood and washed clothes when the snow was very deep all day. There was a child . . . died. They called on me to wash it. Watter would freeze as quick as it touched the child. . . . Our stalk [stock] was so poor we had to leave them" on the range with Lucy's fifteen-year-old son Charlie. "On new years day the frost was so thick in the air we could hardley see the lead horses on our Wagons. . . . One day we onley traveled one mile."

After three months the party arrived at the Mormon settlement of Allen's Camp on the Little Colorado River. Roberta wrote that "the water in the river was so muddy that a barrel full of it left overnight would produce only about six inches of water clear enough to use for culinary purposes." Five times flash floods washed away the dams constructed by the Allen's Camp United Order.

William became so discouraged that one day, according to Roberta, he "saddled up his horse, bade Lucy good-bye and told her there must be a better place in Arizona and if there was he would find it." Commented Lucy, "Some was tried with this, and said he was going to postitise."

Then three-year-old George fell sick. "I did all I could with medicen and also with faith," Lucy wrote.

> My prairs did not seem to be herd but sevral times each day I went away from my wagon in secret and prayed. . . . Often had the Elders administer but it seemed they had no faith. . . . On the morning of July 6th '78 I was so deep in sorrow it seemed I could not bare it any longer. I went out in some brush out of site and asked my Father in Heven to take him home for I could not bare it any longer. My burden was hevier then I could bare. That prair was simple but from my hart. I went to him. He breathed a few times and passed a way so sweetley. My own hands made his clothes, dressed him, fixed some paint and painted his coffin. In

one hour after he passed away his Father came. Had been gon three weeks. Had not herd from us or us from him. I truley was thankfull when he came.

The next day, they drove five miles to Saint Joseph and buried their little child. On July 19 William moved his family to Silver Creek. When they arrived, Roberta reported, "all who were able jumped out of the wagons, rushed to the stream, bathed their faces and drank the first clear water they had since they left their home in Beaver." When William and Lucy later met Elder Erastus Snow, who supervised the Mormon colonies in the area, "William told him what he had done and Elder Snow said, 'I wish we had hundreds just like you.'" Then the apostle proposed the new settlement be named after the two of them; thus Snowflake, Arizona, received its name.

But Lucy's initial enthusiasm for Snowflake was tempered by the spring winds. In her 1896 diary, for example, she wrote:

> Monday, March 2, the wind blows all the time day and part of the time nights and I feel nearly sick.
> Tuesday, April 14, the wind it blows night and day, it is just fearful, The sand drifts like snow. . . . It seems lonely and dreary when the wind blows.
> Thursday, April 16, all well but the Wind gets worse and worse, night and day.
> Saturday, April 18 [William] and John came home this morning. The Wind was so bad Thursday they laid up all day and could not travel. The wind blows very little today which is so nice. I cleaned up all the rooms and had a bath and am going to town.
> Sunday, April 19, today is fearfull the Wind blows so bad.
> Thursday, April 30, this ends the month and I dont beleave there has been one day that the wind did not blow. It has damaged the crops and covered them with sand, filled up the ditches, and made it very unpleasant. [Only] our Hevenly Father nows what this wind is for.
> Monday, May 19, I am on the place all alone. It seems like this country is going to blow away.
> Friday, May 15, the wind blows fearful. The sand almost blinds one. The children cant go out to play.

Occasionally depressed by the unremitting wind, Lucy kept busy with close family ties and callings in the Relief Society, Primary, Sunday School, and Religion Class. William served as first counselor in the bishopric for thirty-five years.

When federal prosecutions for plural marriage reached into Arizona, William declined several broad hints by the sheriff that he could avoid arrest. Instead, he served six months in the penitentiary at Yuma, returning in good spirits and "so fat . . . he had to ware Osmers Pants." (Osmer was their stout son.) Lucy recorded with pride that the Relief Society planned a combination coming-out and birthday party for William: "Sent invertations to all the setlments around, had such nice picknick, esays, songs, speeches, a sketch of his life," complete with a band, and "you never saw a purson so surprised in your life."

Lucy's autobiography and journal provide illuminating details of early Arizona life that would otherwise be lost. Among the routine activities she chronicled one spring were: whitewashing the house; gardening and irrigating; gleaning wool from carcasses along the trail followed by the sheepmen, then picking, washing, and carding it to make a mattress; making underwear, shirts, and carpet rags; tending grand-children; and preparing meals for her husband and growing sons. On one occasion she set down her day's tasks, which were typical of Arizona pioneer women generally: "I will just write my morning chores. Get up, turn out my chickens, draw a pail of watter, watter hot beds, make a fire, put potatoes to cook, brush and sweep half inch of dust off floor, . . . feed three litters of chickens, then mix bisquits, get breakfast, milk besides work in the house and this morning had to go half mile after calves. This is the way of life on the farm."

Lucy's pioneering life was not easy. Five of her thirteen children died in infancy or childhood, and Lucy herself died at fifty-five. Still, the struggle for survival did not absorb all of her energy or prevent spiritual fulfillment: "William and me fasted and went to fast meeting. Had a very good meeting. Un-common good one. Such a good spirrit there. The Sisters had a good testimoney meeting in the afternoon. Twenty two pressant. I presided as Sister West was absent. It is a nice day and all is well."

Chapter 9

Edward Bunker: Living the United Order

Edward Bunker, the youngest of Silas and Hannah Berry Bunker's nine children, was born on 1 August 1822 in Atkinson, Maine. As a teenager, he later wrote, "a spirit of unrest [took] possession of me and I longed to get away." With their parents' permission, Edward and his brother Sabin visited their brothers, Nahum in Massachusetts, and Alfred in Connecticut, where they spent the summer of 1841.

"In the fall my brother-in-law John Berry came along and wanted me to go to Wisconsin with him to see the country. Alfred was away from home at the time, but I packed my trunk and left for the west without bidding him goodbye, and never saw him again." When they reached Cleveland, Edward and John found the lakes had frozen over, blocking their passage to Wisconsin. Waiting for spring, they decided to visit friends in nearby Kirtland, where they chanced to meet Martin Harris. Though he had left the Church several years before, Martin still bore a strong testimony of the Book of Mormon. He "invited us to his house, where we went and heard him bear his testimony to the truth of the Book of Mormon."

Edward and John both read the book and Parley P. Pratt's *Voice of Warning*. John went to Pittsburgh to work, while Edward found employment in Cleveland, attended meetings of the Church, became converted and was baptized in April 1845. "Then I knew why it was that I had been led from my father's house and left my dear old mother, whom I loved so dearly."

That same spring, Edward and John visited friends in Wisconsin who had heard that the Mormons practiced polygamy. Edward, who like most Latter-day Saints at the time had not been instructed in the principle of plural marriage, told them "it was only a slur and a false statement."

In July Edward arrived in Nauvoo with a letter of introduction to Elder George A. Smith, who suggested the young man might find employment working on the temple. This was the year after Joseph Smith's death, and the Saints were still clinging to their city, desperately working to complete the sacred edifice. He made a dollar a week as a laborer, and paid tithing on every cent. "I paid my tithing from the day I was baptized—every tenth day and [even a] tenth of the worth of my clothes." He also worked on the Nauvoo House, cut hay and threshed grain, made flour barrels, and served in the Nauvoo Legion.

During the final days before the evacuation of Nauvoo, Edward worked in Montrose, Iowa, where he met Emily Abbott. They were endowed and married in the Nauvoo Temple by John Taylor in February 1846, the day before Elder Taylor crossed the river to join the Saints at Sugar Creek. Edward and Emily soon followed with the main body of Saints and traveled halfway across Iowa to help settle Garden Grove.

"With the help of brother Steward, a young man who had just been married, I bought a log cabin of one room. We put a roof on it and chucked it, but it was minus doors, floors or windows. We moved our wives into it and I went to Missouri with the intention of earning money enough to buy a team and wagon."

In Missouri, Edward heard that the government had requested the Mormons to raise 500 men for the war with Mexico. "I did not believe it, but the Spirit of the Lord directed me to go home. So the following Saturday, with [a] side of bacon slung over my shoulder, I started for home, thirty miles distant. As I neared my destination I met some brethren hunting stock and they confirmed the report." Brigham Young had called for "all the single men and those that could be spared to come to the bluffs, 140 miles distant." At church the next day, Edward was one of the first to volunteer. On Tuesday he started out for Council Bluffs, where he joined the Mormon Battalion.

At Fort Leavenworth the men were issued weapons and provisions; then they marched to Santa Fe. "I was detailed as assistant teamster to Hyrum Judd," Edward wrote. "By so doing I did not have to carry my gun and knapsack and was exempt from guard duty." From Santa Fe, the battalion marched to Tucson, San Diego, and finally to Los Angeles, where Edward finished out the remaining six months of his hitch.

Discharged in July 1847, Edward and many other battalion members traveled north to Sutter's Mill, and then east to the Salt Lake Valley, arriving on 16 October 1847. After a short rest, he and other battalion members whose families were still in Iowa resumed their journey.

It was late in the season when they reached the Platte River. Ice floes prevented their crossing and a heavy snowstorm soon commenced, forcing them to camp all day. Their food gone, they devoured a pair of rawhide saddle bags which Edward had brought from California. The next morning, with ten inches of snow on the ground, they searched for a passable crossing. When one of the mules fell into the icy water, it had to be killed "and was all eaten up except the lights [lungs]." Finally, on December 18, the weary men reached Winter Quarters. Edward spent the night with his companions, unaware that Emily and eleven-month-old Edward, Jr., had moved from Garden Grove to Winter Quarters and were living just a short distance away.

After a joyful reunion, Edward began preparations for the trek west. He found temporary work in Missouri, then moved his family, Emily's mother, and her two small boys to the Mormon settlement on Mosquito Creek, Iowa. There he raised corn to purchase a yoke of oxen for his mother-in-law, who emigrated to Utah in 1849. Edward was finally able to outfit his own family for the trip the following year.

In Ogden, Edward built a three-room log house at Canfield Creek and was set apart as a member of the first Weber Stake high council by Brigham Young and Heber C. Kimball. Edward also served on Ogden's first city council.

On 26 June 1852 Edward entered the principle he once considered "a slur and a false statement." He acted as proxy for the husband as his neighbor, Sarah Ann Browning Lang, was sealed for eternity to her deceased husband. Edward then married Sarah Ann "for time." Sarah Ann, who had two daughters by William Lang, eventually bore seven children to Edward.

In August 1852 Orson Pratt delivered the first public discourse on the principle of plural marriage, defending it as ordained by God and protected by the U.S. Constitution. In October approximately seventy men were called on missions. Edward was assigned to Great Britain. He and his companions started immediately, "and took with us the first publication of the Revelation on Celestial Marriage which was sent to the nations of the earth." In England Edward was appointed to preside over the Bristol Conference. Three months later he was appointed to preside over the Sheffield, Bradford, and Lincolnshire conferences. Then followed a year of presiding in Scotland before he was released in 1856 to return with 500 emigrants and missionaries.

Landing in New York, the company boarded trains for Saint Louis, then took river boats up the Mississippi to Iowa City, where Edward was appointed to lead a handcart company of Welsh converts across the plains. "Very few of the Welsh could speak English," he observed, adding in understatement, "This made my burden very heavy. . . . We were short of provisions all the way and would have suffered for food had not supplies reached us from the valley."

Other companies that had started a little later, were not so fortunate. Edward and his company reached the valley on 2 October 1856. Three days later Brigham Young addressed the Saints in general conference and called for volunteers to rush to the aid of a thousand handcart pioneers stranded in snow-storms on the plains. Before they could be rescued, two hundred perished.

84

Exhausted and suffering from rheumatism, Edward returned to his family in Ogden. For his wives and children, it was none too soon. Grasshoppers had ravaged the crops, and in the course of the hard winter forty of their cattle died.

Edward was called as bishop of the Ogden Second Ward, a position he occupied for five years.

In the spring of 1861, Edward married Mary M. McQuarrie and in the fall responded to a call to help colonize southwestern Utah. Emily, pregnant with her seventh child, and Mary accompanied Edward and the children to Toquerville. Sarah, expecting her third child by Edward, joined them the following year, and then Edward settled her on a farm in Clover Valley, Nevada. In the fall of 1862, Edward was called to preside as bishop of the Santa Clara, Utah, Ward.

A small, hard-working man with a mild, pleasant face, who believed in practical Christianity, Edward Bunker was well-suited for the office of bishop; but presiding over the Santa Clara Ward was a difficult assignment. The hot, dry climate, coupled with periodic droughts and flash floods, discouraged colonists and impeded growth. "We endured many privations and hardships on account of dry seasons and loss of crops," he wrote. "I was obliged to haul my breadstuffs from the north for several years. . . . Had it not been for the liberality of our brethren in the north our southern settlement would have suffered severely."

When the Panic of 1873 struck, nearby Nevada mines were shut down, throwing Santa Clara miners out of work and cutting off a major market for southern Utah produce. Edward relocated Mary and her family in Panguitch, Utah.

When Brigham Young arrived in Saint George to spend the winter, he found the region in serious need of economic revitalization. The resources of the communities had been depleted, and the settlers were nearly destitute. He suggested a United Order be formed to organize the work force more productively and to distribute the proceeds equitably. Under such an arrangement, he said, they "would never have to buy anything; they would make and raise all they would eat, drink, and wear, and always have something to sell and bring in money, to help to increase their comfort and pleasure."

On the President's recommendation, Bishop Bunker organized the Santa Clara United Order. He dedicated all he had to the Order and worked energetically to make it successful, but some members failed to adhere to the Order's principles, and it was discontinued after one year. Bishop Bunker received back his teams and wagons but "not . . . a pound of hay, grain, flour or cotton, with twenty in the family. Be assured this was a dark day for myself and family." After twelve years as bishop of the Santa Clara Ward, Edward "resigned on account of poor health, not having sufficient resources to keep my family together."

But Edward Bunker was committed to the idea of a community based on economic cooperation, equality, and justice. "We had seen in Santa Clara," he wrote, "the necessity and blessings of the United Order." By the blessing of "the Spirit of the Lord," he declared, "we will found a community fully committed to its principles."

So in January 1877, with Brigham Young's permission, Edward, his wives Emily and Sarah Ann, their children, and a few close friends set out for a new site on the Virgin River, fifty miles southwest of Saint George. Reaching the area previously known as Mesquite Flat, the pioneers gathered together in a circle with arms interlocked and bowed their heads as Bishop Bunker dedicated the land to the Lord. As he prayed, he let wheat fall through the fingers of one hand and soil from their new land through the other. Thus, the community of Bunkerville (so named at Brigham Young's suggestion) was established.

The next day, the colonists began digging a four-foot-wide canal to carry water two miles from the Virgin River to the farm lands. Two weeks later the ditch was complete. The land was cleared of mesquite, rabbit brush, arrow weed and creosote, and over twenty acres of sandy soil were leveled and planted in wheat.

In February thirty-two acres of alfalfa and corn were planted. In March the canal was extended another mile and grapevines and vegetables were set out. In April they planted fourteen acres of cotton, and in June, seven acres of sorghum cane. A dam was constructed to store precious irrigation water, but disaster struck in August when a flash flood broke through. Only quick action by the colonists, who hastily repaired the dam, saved the crops.

The Virgin River water was alkaline, silty, hard, and foul. Occasionally it went on a rampage. As one of Bishop Bunker's daughters wrote, it "gave us no end of trouble, washing out our dams, filling up our ditches, and washing away the land. To cross it, the teams must rest before starting across, then by whipping across quickly to prevent going down in the quicksand."

The women worked in the fields as well as keeping house and gardening. According to one resident, Juanita Brooks, grain was reaped with a cradle, threshed with a flail and by driving cattle over it on a clay floor, and chaffed "by taking the grain in pans, holding it high, and letting it fall on canvas. A breeze would blow the chaff away." In 1878 the harvest was made more efficient when a thresher arrived from California.

The yield was good in 1877 and 1878, and by the end of the second year Bunkerville had a cotton gin, a molasses mill, and a flour mill, all hydro-powered. When a ward was organized, Edward was appointed bishop, with Edward, Jr., and Myron Abbott as counselors. Bishop Bunker reported to a conference in Saint George that the fifteen families of his settlement had produced 450 bushels of wheat, 600 gallons of molasses, and 12,000 pounds of cotton in 1877; and that in 1878 they had produced 1,600 bushels of wheat, 30,000 pounds of cotton, and 1,600 gallons of molasses, and had also raised melons, squash, and other vegetables.

Each family contributed its cattle, teams and wagons, tools, and other supplies to the Order. The land was owned and farmed collectively. Residents ate at a common dining table and gathered together for prayer morning and evening. The women rotated the chores of cooking, washing, ironing, and mending. All drew on the community storehouse according to their particular needs.

The settlers' sense of community was heightened by their common poverty. For although their fields were mercifully productive the first years, much of the produce had to be bartered for clothing, and other supplies. The first houses were temporary shelters with dirt floors and constructed with light lumber.

Infestations of flies and mosquitoes brought malaria; and the heat, said Juanita Brooks, was "the kind that thickens the whites of eggs left in the coop and that makes lizards, scurrying from the shelter of one little bush to another, flip over on their backs and blow their toes." Life in Bunkerville was an unending struggle for survival.

After survival, however, construction of a schoolhouse-meetinghouse had top priority. Completed in 1879, the adobe structure had two glass windows—the first in the village—and a flagstone roof. For twenty years it was the center of community life, housing education, worship, recreation, and civic gatherings.

In a few years the regional economy recovered, and Bunkerville stabilized. Bishop Bunker appraised the United Order as "highly crowned with success." It was remarkably self-sustaining, and united its fifteen families in mutual helpfulness.

But to some, growth and progress seemed more compatible with individual enterprise. So in 1879 the Order was revised to include only those willing to put all they owned into the Order, "that there may be no conflicting interest outside the order." Detailed "By Laws of the Bunkerville United Order" were instituted to implement the law of consecration and stewardship. All property of participating members was turned over to the Order, appraised, entered as capital stock, and then redistributed as stewardships. All "increase" was brought to the communal storehouse for distribution according to need, as determined by a committee of four. But according to Saint George stake records, it soon became apparent that "some stewardships . . . were gathering and laying up in abundance, while others, through carelessness and bad management, were wasting the means of the Company, each year being increasing in debt. This was very unsatisfactory to those whose ambition was to accumulate, at least, the necessaries of life."

Dissatisfaction grew during the harvest of 1880, and Bishop Bunker became increasingly irritated. One member noted that "there was a bad spirit manifested by the Bishop" at council meeting. "He felt like cursing everybody but his own family. At meeting today he felt the same though gave some good instruction on the Word of Wisdom."

Apparently in an effort to adjust the program to reward the industrious and strengthen the economy, the bishop proposed that each steward be entitled to draw up to 80 percent of his labor; the rest would be retained for the common good. But the proposal proved divisive and it was decided to disband the Order.

Still, for many years new homes were built, crops harvested, and cheese manufactured communally.

There was something grand and enduring about the Bunkerville United Order. Some of Nevada's most distinguished citizens grew up there. Leavitts, Pulsiphers, Bunkers, Abbotts, Earls, Coxs, and other Bunkerville families continue to contribute to the religious, economic, and political life of Nevada. Two of the West's finest historians, LeRoy Hafen and Juanita Brooks, grew up in Bunkerville. With only limited employment opportunities, Bunkerville exported many of its talented young people to towns like Moapa, Glendale, and Logandale in nearby valleys.

In 1901 white-haired Bishop Bunker set out with Emily and three children to help found the Mormon colony at Colonia Morelos, Mexico. Within a month of his arrival there, he died, leaving behind a spiritual monument of idealism and practical Christianity.

Chapter 10

Lemuel H. Redd:
Down the Chute
to San Juan

Lemuel Redd was fourteen when he drove his father's ox-team from Winter Quarters to the Salt Lake Valley in 1850. The family first settled in Provo, then in Spanish Fork, where Lemuel's father John built a large flour mill and served as counselor in the branch presidency. In January 1856 Lemuel married Keziah Jane Butler. They would eventually have thirteen children.

In February 1856 John Redd was called to the recently established mission at Las Vegas. But since his wife had died in 1853 and John had the responsibility of two teenage sons, Lemuel and Keziah went in his place. They apparently arrived in Las Vegas with a company of new missionaries on June 15.

Las Vegas ("the meadows") was an outpost situated on a small spring in the middle of the Nevada desert. It consisted of an adobe fort 150 feet on each side, with walls two feet thick, 14 feet high on one side, and 9 feet high on the other three sides. Construction of a new fort had just begun when Lemuel and Keziah arrived. There was also a large corral and stockyard. Fruit trees had been planted, and when Lemuel and Keziah arrived, the missionaries harvested their barley, wheat, and oats, and planted corn and beans. A guard was posted day and night to watch for thieves or hostile Indians.

90

Fort Las Vegas served as a resting place for travelers on their way to and from California. But its primary purpose was religious. In 1855, the first year of operations, the Las Vegas missionaries baptized sixty-four Indians, including Chief Owntump of the Paiutes and a number of Quoeech Indians. In addition to teaching and baptizing, the missionaries gave Indian converts "Christian" names such as Alma, Benjamin, Joshua, George, and Albert, and tried to teach them new methods of farming—with a modicum of success.

Shortly after the arrival of Lemuel and Keziah, the mission president announced plans to work a lead mine in the mountains about thirty-five miles to the southwest. The lead they mined would be bartered for foodstuffs to support the mission. Although several missionaries were opposed to beginning the work in mid-summer, on July 29 Lemuel and fourteen others were assigned to leave for the mine.

After just a month at the mine, John Redd requested Lemuel be released because he was needed at home. Lemuel and Keziah returned to Spanish Fork. In December their first child, Lemuel, Jr., was born.

In January 1858 Lemuel and Keziah consecrated to the Church their lot and house in Spanish Fork, twenty acres of farm land, one ox, three cows and two heifers, two sheep, one pig, a rifle, forty bushels of wheat, ten bushels of corn, eight bushels of potatoes, miscellaneous garden vegetables and 250 pounds of pork—total value, $829.50. In April a second child was born; in June, John Redd died and Lemuel assumed responsibility for his younger brother Benjamin.

In 1862 Brigham Young called the Redds to help settle New Harmony, southwest of Cedar City, Utah. There Lemuel served on the county commission and was a director of the Kanarra Cattle and Sheep Company. In 1866 he married seventeen-year-old Sariah Louise Chamberlain, who would eventually become the mother of fourteen children. In 1870 he bought John D. Lee's farm on the headwaters of Ash Creek and enlarged the brick house so that each of his two wives would have her own apartment. When New Harmony entered the United Order in 1874, Lemuel became its vice-president and secretary. He also pulled teeth, was a practical veterinarian, and served as ward chorister.

A year and a half after the death of Brigham Young, President John Taylor began urging Latter-day Saints to settle the usable farm and grazing land of southeastern Utah's San Juan region while it was still available. Latter-day Saint settlements could help establish friendly relations with the Indians and do missionary work among them.

Moreover, the wild and remote area of San Juan was becoming a refuge for bank and train robbers, cattle rustlers, and other desperadoes. "Solid citizens" were needed to establish law and order.

In April 1879, under instructions from the First Presidency, Bishop Silas S. Smith of Paragoonah led an expedition in search of a suitable location for a proposed settlement. Proceeding south into Arizona, then east through Navajo and Hopi territory, they eventually turned north again and arrived in the Four Corners region of southeastern Utah in June. There they selected two or three possible sites near present-day Montezuma and erected a few crude shelters for the settlers who would remain behind to make improvements. Water had been scarce on their route to Montezuma, and the Indians resented their intrusion, so the explorers decided to look for a better route for the main company to follow. They went north through Moab, then west to Paragoonah, completing their nine-hundred-mile circle in mid-September.

It was late in the season. If the pioneers took the five-hundred-mile northern route they would not arrive at their new homes until mid-winter. The southern route was also long, and dangerous. The only solution seemed to be a shortcut directly east from Escalante. If they could find a way through the treacherous terrain along the Colorado River, the explorers estimated the direct route could be negotiated in six weeks.

Assured that the journey was feasible, eighty families from five counties began to converge on the base camp forty miles east of Escalante. By late November Lemuel and members of his family arrived. Silas S. Smith arrived on the 27th and surveyed the situation. The main obstacle seemed to be a 2,000-foot cliff fifteen miles away which they would have to descend before the company could cross the Colorado and continue to Montezuma. Scouts located a narrow slit in the cliff which might be widened with blasting powder. Silas returned to Salt Lake City to obtain appropriations from the First Presidency and the territorial legislature to purchase the explosives. Four scouts, including Lemuel Redd, were sent on to blaze a trail from the river to Montezuma.

Riding two horses, with a mule and Lemuel's burro as pack animals, the four scouts started out on 17 December 1879. They had supplies for eight days. Their map indicated Montezuma was seventy miles due east and they assumed they could average twenty miles a day.

The first day they got down the cliff and arrived at the Colorado River. The next day they crossed the river and spotted a flock of fourteen mountain sheep. Soon they were in unexplored country. Box canyons and broken terrain slowed their progress. They discovered abandoned Indian cliff dwellings and slept in them several nights. An Indian trail led them in the right direction, but on the seventh day an eight-inch snowstorm obliterated the trail.

On Christmas Eve the weather turned bitter-cold. Lemuel and his companions ate the last of their rations. Lost and without food, the scouts almost gave up hope of seeing their families again, but then from a small knoll they spotted the Blue Mountains, an important landmark. Three days later they arrived at the present site of Bluff, where they found a Mormon family which had recently arrived from Colorado. Eagerly the four starving explorers consumed all the meat that the settlers could spare and a large batch of biscuits. The next day they continued to Montezuma where they found the inhabitants eating their seed wheat. "Our first meal of chopped wheat would shame a dose of salts in its purging propensities," wrote one of the scouts.

Lemuel and his companions began their return trip on 31 December 1879 and arrived back at the cliffs on January 10 after twenty-four harrowing days. They found shifts of forty-seven men working from dawn to dark widening the crack in the mountain wall while another thirty men worked on the road below.

Finally, after weeks of work the first wagon was lowered down the Hole-in-the-Rock chute, which has been described as a mine with the top blown off. Actually, it is not a "hole" at all, but a narrow steep cut in the west wall of Glen Canyon. First came a sheer drop of almost one hundred feet, then a little less steep decline of another three hundred feet. Steps had been carved into the sandstone for footing. With ropes tied to the wagons and held by twenty men and boys, each wagon was slowly guided down the "hole." Jagged rocks tore at the feet of the horses and cattle. Slowly, painfully, the entire company of 230 persons, their wagons, provisions, and livestock made their way down to the river below.

The remainder of the route, punctuated by long stretches of broken terrain, occasional chutes, and frequent sand mires, took Lemuel and his family through one of the most forbidding regions in Western America. As one settler later wrote, "It's the roughest country you or anybody else ever seen; it's nothing in the world but rocks and holes, hills and hollows. The mountains are just one solid rock as smooth as an apple."

After nearly six months of constant road building and travel, they reached San Juan Hill. This last obstacle almost proved too much for the worn-out teams, which had been weakened by a long winter of hard work and insufficient feed. Charlie Redd, one of young Lemuel's sons, graphically described the last effort:

> Aside from the Hole-in-the-Rock itself, this was the steepest crossing on the journey. Here again seven span of horses were used, so that when some of the horses were on their knees, fighting to get up to find a foothold, the still-erect horses could plunge upward against the grade. On the worst slopes the men were forced to beat their jaded animals into giving all they had. After several pulls, rests, and pulls, many of the horses took to spasms and near-convulsions, so exhausted were they. By the time most of the outfits were across, the worst stretches could easily be identified by the dried blood and matted hair from the

94

forelegs of the struggling teams. My father [young Lemuel] was a strong man, and reluctant to display emotion; but whenever in later years the full pathos of San Juan Hill was recalled either by himself or by someone else, the memory of such bitter struggles was too much for him and he wept.

Finally, on 5 April 1880 the main company reached the lower San Juan. When they sighted their valley for the first time, their emotions were so near the surface that in order to keep from crying with relief, they broke out singing "The Latter-day Work Rolls On." Too exhausted to negotiate the remaining eighteen miles to Montezuma, they founded Bluff, a city which has never had more people than the two hundred who originally settled it one hundred years ago.

Three times in the difficult years that followed—in 1882, 1884, and 1897—the residents of Bluff petitioned Church authorities for permission to abandon the colony, but each time they were visited by General Authorities who encouraged them to "carry on." Lemuel Redd returned to New Harmony, and later went to the Mormon colony at Juarez, Mexico, where he died in 1910. Young Lemuel remained in Bluff with his family, where he served many years as bishop and then as president of San Juan Stake. He also was an assessor and tax collector, organizer and manager of the San Juan Ward Co-op, county superintendent of schools, delegate to the Utah Constitutional Convention, and owner of the Dark Canyon Cattle Company.

Lemuel Redd's healthy mixture of faith and realistic expectation is illustrated by an incident during a year of drouth when a group of Saints asked him, "President Redd, don't you think we should pray for rain?"

"Yes, yes, by all means pray for rain," he answered, "but remember, brethren, this is a very dry country."

Chapter 11

Chauncey West: Nineteenth Century Teenager

It was New Year's Eve 1895. Chauncey West and his friends gathered at the Brigham City court house. It seemed the entire community had come to hear

> the large bell . . . strike the old year's ending. At the last stroke we, or our party, numbering about twelve young Ladies and Gentlemen holding the ropes, started the bells ringing the Old year out and the new year in.
>
> Later we . . . went over to My cousins and . . . played tiddy winks untill almost two o'clock. I retired at two o'clock, and arose on the first day, 1895 at 6:30 o'clock in the morning, studied Oratory, by Bulcher, at 8:30 went to work at the B. C. M. & M. A. Store, helped straighten the goods that had been in their late fire as published in my book of rememberances. In the evening went to the New Years Ball, accompanied by L.C. Snow Uncle, Frouie, and Claudie my Sisters. I had a very nice time and enjoyed myself. Danced with Miss Annie Rich one time, Miss Amelia Graehle 1, Miss Hattie Keever 3 times, Miss Flossie Snow, Mrs. Stowl, Miss Ella Jensen, Miss Claudia 3, Miss Tennie Snow. Went home and retired with my Uncle who was my guest from S.L. City—L.C. Snow at two o'clock.

At eighteen, LeRoi C. Snow was Chauncey's closest friend, and though they were about the same age, also his uncle. When

LeRoi's father, Lorenzo Snow, was called to be president of the Salt Lake Temple, they moved from Brigham City to Salt Lake City, where LeRoi became temple librarian. As often as he could, LeRoi boarded the Utah Northern and made the fifty-mile railroad trip to visit his home town friends.

Chauncey was a newcomer to Brigham City. He had grown up in Butte and Anaconda, Montana, where his father was stationed as a railroad conductor. One day a man without a ticket tried to board the train in Colorado. When Chauncey's father tried to stop him, the man pulled a gun and shot him. Chauncey's father was buried in Ogden, Utah. Chauncey, his mother, and two sisters moved to Brigham where they could be close to relatives.

Chauncey was a demon for self-improvement. Even on New Year's Day, after a late night of tiddlywinks, he rose at 6:30 to study before going to work at the Brigham City Merchandise and Mercantile Association. There, Chauncey stocked shelves, sent out advertising fliers, and performed other miscellaneous chores, such as sorting peaches, for $24.50 a month.

In the evenings he attended classes in phonography (shorthand) and civil government, and studied U.S. history at MIA. He also studied phonetics, etymology, geography, oratory, and rhetoric, some of which may have been in connection with the MIA, but much of which seems to have sprung from his own thirst for knowledge. LeRoi loaned him several Church books, including John Taylor's *Mediation and Atonement*, B.H. Roberts's *Succession in the Church*, and the six-volume Chambers encyclopedia. Chauncey himself worked hard to save $10.50 for the two-volume set of Blackstone's *Commentaries*. He devoted many hours to studying this basic legal text, noting "The Latin phrases are the only things that I don't read, although I studied Latin some, I cannot readily read them."

The civil government class was something of a debating society, organized along lines similar to today's Model United Nations. Chauncey was assigned his home state of Montana "to defend hereafter." Since 1895 was the year of Utah's constitutional convention, the class organized a mock convention, where one of the most hotly debated topics was female suffrage. Chauncey championed the cause, and when the matter was put to a vote, "The house was in disorder. The vote stood 21 to 21. The president decided in favor of woman suffrage."

Chauncey was an assiduous record-keeper. He maintained a daily journal, a "book of rememberances," and a "book of my addresses made in public." His humorous accounts of otherwise mundane events make the diary an entertaining record. For example, one morning he wrote,

> at six thirty I was awakened very suddenly by my electric clock and bells.
> I made one jump and landed out of bed on the floor. Then my understanding was clear and I, knowing that if I did not in a minute shut my electric bells off from the strong current, that the batteries would be run down and the neighbors would turn out thinking there was a fire, I jumped spryly in the direction of my electric clock, but I had barely got started toward it in the blind darkness, than I ran against some living thing and turned a summer salt in the air and fell all in a heap and the noise of the gong sounded longer and louder. After I got my understanding I made another attempt, shutting off the electric currant & lighting the lamp, looking for the person that I had fell over, it was a chair.

Chauncey enjoyed Brigham City life, especially the carefree hours with LeRoi Snow and Wallace Boden. One Saturday night, Chauncey and LeRoi "went to Wallace's to retire for the night. We got to wrasteling for the covering and after about two hours of this work, the bed fell down so we had to sleep on the floor the rest of the night. But in all we enjoyed it, to the greatest of our ability."

The next day was Sunday—fast Sunday. Chauncey fasted until noon, "as was required of the members of the sunday school." He was called upon to speak by the Sunday School superintendent, and dutifully recorded the talk in his speech book. After afternoon and evening church services, LeRoi and Wallace went to Chauncey's, where they again "enjoyed our selves fighting for the bed coverings."

But as much as Brigham City's "three musketeers" reveled in raucous horseplay, they also worked at developing cultural skills. When invited to Miss Ada Nickler's home after work (January 2), "we . . . enjoyed our selves with selections on the organ and playing spelling games which were not only amusement but were of an instructive lesson." And the morning after the bedsheet tussle, the three rose at six to discuss the Bible.

Intent on developing physical as well as intellectual strength, Chauncey rose at his usual hour on January 9, "and after pertaking of a lively dumb bell exercise, I felt exceedingly strong and refreshed." Chauncey found fifteen minutes with the Indian clubs and dumb bells would "get my blood in good circulation so I could keep warm, it being a cold, biteing, blistering morning, and rather cold in my room to study for two hours with out a fire."

One day Chauncey paused to reflect on the sights and sounds of a Brigham City winter:

> The sun, although very high and rather low toward the south, shone bright through the [clouds] and made a small effort to rid us of some of [the] winter blanket. Sleighs containing lovers and sweethearts were seen by the dozens, and the sight was a loving one. Fleet horses drawing light cutters were flying past the busy store, the merry bells echoing and reverberating over the frozen snow. In all, this was a beautiful winter day.

Perhaps the most popular form of recreation in the nineteenth century was dancing. Seldom did a month pass without at least one Church-sponsored ball. Chauncey escorted his sisters to the Grand Ball and then returned for Miss Hawes:

> I had a fine time, Going to supper at 12, then returning from Mrs. Boden's Hotel to the dance, or Ball room. We continued dancing until ten minutes to 3, when the Electric lights began to go out. We quickly sent a signal to the Electrician, at the Electric plant, by three shutoffs of the lights, to continue the lights for half an hour. He understanding the City signal, kept the Machinery going for about 45 minutes longer. We abandoned the hall very early in the morning. . . . I got to bed about 4, (after taking Miss Hawes home), being, or experiencing, a very tired sensation such as all Society ball lovers many times experience. You know!

Music was an important part of Chauncey's life. On Saturday, January 12, he worked through the dinner hour,

> in order to get an honorable release to take the musical part in the Sunday School Concert. . . . We met at Mrs. Squires for practice at half past six and at seven we left for the concert. It was a grand success and lasted late in the night. The Brigham orchestra opened, after which we had prayer, and my string and hormonica band of Brigham, consisting of three guitars, one banjo, two hormonicas, of which I played one and led, ended the program with two selections, being well encored and having to play again. I enjoyed the evening very much and going home, the crowd marched and followed our music.

He also sang in the ward choir and frequently went serenading with his friends. One night, "we, numbering five, consisting of guitars, mandolins, banjo and a harmonica, which I played and also led the string band with, we had a glorious time being invited in a number of places to partake of molasses, candy, popcorn, and refreshments of all kinds and descriptions." On another occasion, Chauncey and the boys

> went to serenade the Bells of Brigham thinking that they were about all in bed. But when we serenaded Miss Rich the daughter of Mr. Rich the Brigham Banker, they supprizes us by all coming out on the porch to listen, after which Miss Rich kindly invited us in, but we refused, saying we did not expect to go in, thinking them in bed, but she begged and we strongly refused her kind offer, after which we played her another tune. She ran off and barely before we finished, she brought four glasses of wine. I took my glass, but set it back full untouched.

Chauncey was preparing for a mission. He had been baptized and confirmed on Thursday, 3 January 1895 and six days later, "went to meeting to be ordained a deacon, but after the speaking was over it was so late that it was suggested that we post pone the ordaining of deacons." On January 30, "I went up to be ordained a deacon, but the Bishop did not show up and I, to my sorrow, was again the second time disappointed. I worked in the old shoe factory, sorting peaches." A month later he attended a meeting of teachers and deacons. "I wished to be ordained a deacon but did not know if that privilege would be granted me or not. It was talked over and Mr. L. Jeppson ordained me a Teacher. I was very glad to be

100

ordained as I was into the Aronic Priesthood and intend living a humble life."

LeRoi had given Chauncey a Book of Mormon for Christmas with the stipulation that he read it every fast day. Rarely did he let a week go by without reading at least a few chapters. At the end of January, Chauncey received "a hint of going to Germany on a mission with L.C. Snow in about one year." He studied the Bible and the Book of Mormon, Tullidge's *Life of Joseph Smith,* and various other works. George Graehle tutored him in German. "At all times in the store when I had nothing to do," he wrote, "I would grab my German book and learn a few words."

In early spring Chauncey went fishing with Wallace Boden and Henry Blackburn. A few days later, Chauncey and Wallace "laid on the lawn until late and conversed on astronomy and what could be in the stars that twinkled and sparkled so beautiful away up in the heavens." At times Chauncey seemed to live in an idyllic world. "This is a bright and beautiful morning," he wrote, "and Brigham is laden with blossoms of many colors and shapes. This is the first year of many that I have had such pleasure of seeing and smelling the numberless flowers, and I must confess Brigham is a beautiful city of foliage, flowers and homes, and at present is wrapped in beauty."

The highlight of Chauncey's year came in April when he took the train for Salt Lake with LeRoi. Stopping briefly in Ogden, they visited relatives and the grave of Chauncey's father, then continued on to Salt Lake City. Arriving at 9:30 P.M., LeRoi took Chauncey on a tour of the "electric light works, business college, bicycle school, and Christensen's dancing academy," before retiring for the night at LeRoi's home.

The next day, the sight-seeing continued—ZCMI, the *Deseret News* building, and the hot springs. At general conference, Chauncey saw his uncle George Q. Cannon, his cousin Abraham H. Cannon, his grandfather Lorenzo Snow, and other Church leaders. As for the meeting itself, Chauncey noted only that "one of the apostles, namely Lyman, became so over powered in his speech that he cried."

101

The sixth of April was a special day, a day of beginnings. After a tour of the city and county building,

> I met Grandpa on my way home (to where I were staying), and it was *my* wish that *I* be ordained an *Elder* Of The Church Of Jesus Christ Of Latter-day Saints, this day, it being the sixty-fifth anniversary of the orginazation of the Church.
>
> I got [stake] president R. Clawson's consent, and went to the Temple and was ordained in the Temple an Elder by Grandpa, (the President of the Salt Lake Temple) and LeRoie Snow. 7:30 o'clock.
>
> We then went to the concert in the Tabernacle, given by the choir (Salt Lake City Tabernicle choir numbering about one thousand). The large choir singing, and the immense organ screeching, fairly shook the Tabernicle.
>
> I enjöyed the concert, and was well entertained. After it was over we went out, and the Large World's fair search lights now in the city was turned on us. It was so strong that I would turn my back to it. We watched them (two) for some time, and had them turned on us going home.

Chauncey attended all sessions of general conference, visited the theater, the Deseret Museum, the science building at the University of Utah, and attended a class in "Doctorernal Theology" at the LDS College. Then he and LeRoi had lunch in the temple and were given an extraordinary tour.

> We . . . went in the six towers as far as we could safely get. We almost went to the top of the west middle tower, up past the last strait projection. I never care to be in a nicer place than the Temple. When we came back down I sat in the chair maid for the President of The Temple, (my Grandpa). It was as soft and easy as life could wish to rest upon. I walked over the top of the Temple. We came out after three hours walking and seeing. I went through as thoroughly as anybody and more than visitors and workers.

He returned the temple the following day and was baptized on behalf of fourteen deceased persons. "I then went around in the Temple for a while, and enjoyed myself very much under its holy roof."

On April 10 Chauncey arrived at the temple at 8:50 A.M. and attended a preliminary meeting in the annex. "It was fine. I then prepared myself to go through the Temple. It was the crowdest day that there had ever been in the Temple, I getting

102

through the first one, at about 4:30."

The next morning Chauncey "went through [the temple] for a dead person," in a shorter, six-and-a-half hour session.

On Saturday morning Chauncey and LeRoi went for a bicycle ride with three young ladies:

> The Girls looked very neat in their tight fitting waists and bloomers. I rode along the side of Miss Abbie Wardrobe and enjoyed the trip very much. We returned after about one and a half hours ride with our partners. Then leaving them at home we started for Beck's Hot Springs and had a fine trip. We went around the sloping bicycle track and then returned. We then started for the Fort, namely Fort Douglas. We had a hard ride going up, but coming down, I just sailed.

Then they took the 2:00 P.M. train to "Saltair Beech," toured the magnificent ball rooms, and floated in the salty lake.

After twelve days in Salt Lake City, Chauncey returned to work in Brigham City and decided to take the qualifying examination for public school teachers. "Grandpa . . . was pleased and said, That is right, the store is no place for you." The exam took nine hours. "I have not been over the questions or work that were given for examination for about four years," Chauncey wrote, "and not knowing in time to get to study thoroughly, I may not get a very high percent, but I think I will get a certificate for teaching."

While he waited for the results, Chauncey studied every subject he could to prepare for a teaching career. But when his score arrived, it was "just two percent too low to get the certificate. I regretted it very much. . . . It was my ignorance in regards to the questions asked."

But this setback did not diminish Chauncey's desire to improve. The following Sunday, he spoke in church. "I were also asked by the Superntendant, and aproved by the vote of the Sunday School to administer the Sacrament (with another gentleman) For the following Month. I sang in the choir. I went to meeting in the [Brigham City] Tabernicle and enjoyed it very much. Grandpa spoke. Just before meeting, I being a little early, I wrote in my memmorandum book as many Gems of Noted Orators and Writers that I could think of. I wrote seventeen before meeting began."

It must be conceded that Chauncey West was not a typical young man. His attention to the development of all sides of his personality—intellectual, physical, social, and spiritual—was extraordinary for a young man of any era.

Chauncey was also extraordinary because of his special relationship to "dear old Grandpa," Lorenzo Snow, whom he described as "over 87 years old and spry as can be." On 28 April 1895, the young man had a conversation with his grandfather that he surely never forgot: "Last night Grandpa told me how he came to join the Church and said he had eaten and drunk at the table of Joseph Smith, the seer, translator, interpreter, and prophet. And Grandpa said he knew this church was a true church, and had it direct."

Chauncey wrote little about his family. References to his mother and sisters are rare. But this entry discloses something of the relationship: "This day I made Mamma present of an overcoat, letting her pick out any one she wanted in the store."

It is unfortunate that the only significant source on this remarkable young man covers such a short period of time. But in his six-month diary we have a picture of the possibilities that his time and place presented, and a glimpse of that rare quality of self-motivation that has always distinguished the best of the Latter-day Saints.

3

The Twentieth Century

*S*ome years ago the great Western historian Walter Prescott Webb told the authors, "Mormon history has everything. It is the ideal topic for a historian. It has sacrifice, persecution, great movements across space, pioneering, economic experimentation, political struggle, and religious zeal. And it has a beginning, a middle, and an end."

Webb and some other historians seem to feel that the adjustments associated with the Manifesto and the coming of statehood to Utah ended the distinctiveness of Mormonism. According to this interpretation, Latter-day Saints entered the American mainstream and became virtually indistinguishable from the rest of society.

There is some truth to this view, of course, because changes of policy did occur, and in many respects the Mormons, tired of constant harrassment, welcomed the "respectability" of full-fledged citizenship. But the adjustment was far from an abandonment of principle; it was a creative adjustment that enabled the Saints to pursue the main goals of their theological and ecclesiastical program.

Too much that is genuinely exciting has occurred in the twentieth century to conclude that Mormon history ended with the nineteenth.

From 1840 to the present, one or more members of the Richards family has served almost continuously in the leading councils of the Church. George F. Richards is an especially interesting link in this great chain because so many advancements were made during his lifetime (1861-1950).

From the very beginning, Latter-day Saints have been theologically and culturally interested in the American Indian. Helen Sekaquaptewa is a Hopi who joined the Church in 1953. Her life before and after baptism illustrates the inspiration and the conflict generated by the traditions of her people as she bridges two cultures.

Though his professional training led philosopher Ephraim E. Ericksen to make a critical evaluation of the Church's theology and programs, his contributions on the YMMIA General Board and in the classroom have had significant impact on modern Mormonism. The contributions of his wife

Edna Clark Ericksen were equally important to the develop-
ment of the Primary's Trail Builder program.

*Following her immigration from Switzerland during
World War II, Margrit Feh Lohner made an unusually
successful adaptation to American society. She became a
prominent member of the YWMIA General Board and general
Church Music Committee. Her enthusiasm for the arts and the
Church has made her an especially effective leader of young
women throughout the Church.*

*As a missionary, T. Edgar Lyon experienced spiritual gifts
which helped sustain his faith throughout his life. Later, as a
mission president in Holland he witnessed the effects of the
Depression and Nazism in Europe. As a seminary and institute
teacher, Ed Lyon earned a rare reputation—that of a devoted
teacher, and, at the same time, a respected scholar.*

Chapter 12

George F. Richards:
A Link in the Chain

The life of George F. Richards spanned pioneer Utah and World War II. He knew Brigham Young, who died when George was sixteen, and Presidents John Taylor, Wilford Woodruff, Lorenzo Snow, Joseph F. Smith, and Heber J. Grant. His life illustrates as well as any one life can the course of the Church from the times of horse and buggy to the age of commercial air travel.

George was born on 23 February 1861 in Farmington, Utah, to Franklin D. Richards and Nanny Longstroth. The Richards family had a long tradition of Church service. Franklin D.'s uncle, Willard Richards, had been in Carthage Jail with Joseph and Hyrum Smith when they were martyred. Later, Willard served as a counselor to Brigham Young. As Church Historian he supervised the research and compilation which later resulted in the multi-volume *History of the Church.*

When Willard Richards died, Brigham Young counseled his nephew and fellow apostle Franklin D. Richards to fulfill the levirate law by marrying his uncle's widows and assuming responsibility for his families. Franklin D. already had five living wives and many children, but on 6 March 1857 he was sealed for time and eternity to a sixth wife and was sealed for time only to Willard's four widows. (Two weeks later he also married another wife.) One of the widows was Nanny

Longstroth, who was to become the mother of George F. Richards and grandmother of LeGrand Richards.

Plural marriage required the greatest cooperation and understanding from all partners and often placed heavy economic burdens on the families. Nanny Longstroth lived in Farmington, fifteen miles north of Franklin D.'s home in Salt Lake City. When George F. was born, his father's time and attention were necessarily divided among his several families, his duties as a prominent leader in the territorial legislature, and his Church assignments. When George F. was five, his father left on a three-year mission to England, where he presided over the European missions. On his return, Brigham Young assigned him to preside over Weber Stake, and he moved to Ogden, twenty miles north of Farmington.

So at an early age George F. was needed to help provide for his mother, brother and sister. He worked hard, but occasionally when cutting wood in the canyons, he would rise before sunup to be in town in time to play an afternoon baseball game.

In the nineteenth century it was not unusual for children to be baptized at a relatively advanced age. Nor had the age of ordination to the Aaronic Priesthood been fixed. (In fact, most holders of the Aaronic Priesthood were adult men.) Thus, George F. Richards was baptized when he was twelve and apparently never was ordained to the Aaronic Priesthood. Instead, his father ordained him an elder at the age of fifteen. On the same day, he received his endowments in the Endowment House and was soon called on a stake mission.

While he was still a teenager George F. attended the University of Deseret (later the University of Utah) in Salt Lake City and at the age of twenty graduated in English literature. The following year he married Alice Robinson of Farmington. They eventually had fifteen children, thirteen of whom lived to maturity.

In 1885, when George F. was twenty-four, the Richards moved to Fielding, a farming community in northern Utah. Three years later they moved to Uncle Abram Doremus's ranch in Tooele, west of Salt Lake City. Their four-room house was

110

graced with a front porch and included a cellar and attic but no inside toilet facilities. "We used to bathe in a round galvanized tub with water heated on the kitchen stove," their son Joel remembered.

About the time Utah became a state (1896), George F. bought a house and farmland in Tooele. The two-story adobe house (two rooms upstairs and two rooms downstairs) soon proved inadequate, so the family moved into a shed while it was torn down and a new one built. The new house was one of the finest in Tooele. When running water, electric lights, and indoor toilet facilities were installed, the family was "in our seventh heaven."

George F. and his sons plowed the land with a handplow and planted grain with a horse-drawn drill. Eventually they purchased a header pulled by four horses, which harvested wheat in a twelve-foot swath. After finishing their own grain, the Richards family worked on their neighbors' harvest, taking wheat as payment. They cut the alfalfa with a mowing machine, windrowed it with a horse-drawn rake, and, when it was dry, loaded it onto a hayrack to be transported home where it was stacked with a derrick.

George F.'s sons knew what it meant to work. They planted, weeded, and harvested crops, and cut and hauled wood from the canyons. When their father started a lumber and implement business, they loaded and unloaded lumber, kept the books, and waited on customers.

One summer Stephen L. Richards joined his cousin LeGrand and his uncle George F. during the harvest. At noon the three future apostles crawled under the hay rake, ate their lunch, and conversed about the gospel.

George F. made it a point to talk to his sons as they worked side by side. "While we were hoeing weeds out of the corn field," LeGrand wrote, "Father would ask us questions about the gospel. . . . I can remember to this day one of his questions: 'What is the gospel?' and our discussion of that question has remained with me all these years."

Not so enjoyable was wash day. "I used to dread wash day every week," Joel recalled.

111

It seemed to be my job to help Mother with the washing. . . . The first washer we had was operated with a handle pushed forward and backward to operate the dolly inside the washer. The next one was a rocker type that was rocked like a cradle, and when I got tired of rocking it by hand I would sit on the porch railing and rock it with my feet. Then someone invented a washer with a wheel that was turned to operate the dolly and we got one. This was an improvement over the others but still it got awful tiresome turning that wheel for all those batches of clothes, and then Mother would have to scrub the clothes on a scrubbing board to get them clean.

Eventually, Joel figured out a way to hook up his bicycle to the washer so he could turn the washer wheel by peddling.

In addition to farming and business activities, George F. also had civic and church responsibilities. He represented Tooele one term in the Utah Legislature and also served as chairman of the board for the local school district and irrigation company. In 1890 he was set apart as a counselor in the Tooele Stake presidency, and three years later, at the age of thirty-nine, he was ordained a patriarch.

In 1905, to celebrate the centennial anniversary of the birth of Joseph Smith, the Church erected a tall granite monument at Sharon, Vermont. George F. and Alice were invited to accompany President Joseph F. Smith and about twenty-five others on the train to Vermont. They attended the dedication services on December 23 and visited Manchester, Palmyra, Kirtland, and Omaha (Winter Quarters) on the return trip.

Following general conference in April 1906, President Smith called George F. to fill a vacancy in the Quorum of the Twelve Apostles. Two other apostles, Orson F. Whitney and David O. McKay, were called at the same time.

George F. promptly sold his land and business interests in Tooele, moved his family to Salt Lake City, and immersed himself in his responsibilities. Between that conference and the next one in October, George F. attended an average of three stake conferences a month.

George F. Richards was not noted for his oratory but quickly gained the respect of the Saints for his sound counsel and quiet spirituality, qualities that had made him an

112

outstanding father. His first opportunity to address the Saints at conference came in October 1907, eighteen months after his call. He noted the generous outpouring of the Spirit during the conference and the uplifting talks that had been presented. Then he observed, "We have also been edified by the thoughts which have arisen in our minds, as a result of what we have heard. . . . I firmly believe that one of the most fruitful sources of spiritual education lies in the thoughts which arise in our own hearts, perhaps apart and independent of that which we are listening to. We are fed upon the bread of life by the Spirit of the Lord, and I feel that we have been so fed at this conference."

The years of George F. Richards's apostleship, from 1906 to 1950, were years of transition. As he traveled to stake conferences Elder Richards found that some priesthood holders did not belong to a quorum. In 1910 the general priesthood committee on which he served recommended, among other things, scheduling priesthood meetings on Sunday mornings instead of Monday evenings. Three years later the change was approved along with a comprehensive reorganization of the Aaronic Priesthood: ages were established for ordination to deacon, teacher, and priest; their responsibilities were clarified; and courses of study prepared. George F. helped shape the pattern of priesthood activity familiar to most of us today.

George F. inherited an intense interest in Church history from his father. He participated in the discussions which led to the improvement of Temple Square as a center for visitors, the purchase of historic sites in New York, and the commissioning of two sculptures—the Mormon Battalion Monument on the State Capitol grounds and the "This Is the Place Monument" at the mouth of Emigration Canyon.

At the height of World War I Elder Richards was called to preside over the British and European missions. After he told his wife and children they could not go with him, he wrote in his diary, "It broke up my wife's feelings and the children cried with her. My true feelings are that I would naturally shrink from such responsibility and having to leave home and loved ones for such a time as this mission will mean, but having put my hand to the plow there is for me no turning back."LeGrand had just returned from presiding over the Netherlands Mission, but fortunately his son George F., Jr. and his daughter-in-law were able to accompany Elder Richards to his post in Liverpool. It was a traumatic situation for a mission president. The number of missionaries had been drastically reduced and proselyting virtually ceased until the end of the war.

When George F. returned to Salt Lake City in the spring of 1919, Heber J. Grant was the new President of the Church. Joseph F. Smith had died on 19 November 1918, just eight days after the armistice had been signed. Elder Richards was given his first office, a room in the new Church Administration Building, which had been completed just before his departure in 1916. Symbolic of the expanded organization of the Church, the building at 47 East South Temple became the scene of Elder Richards's daily work for more than thirty years.

In 1921 Elder Richards and his wife Alice were called to be president and matron of the Salt Lake Temple. During his sixteen-year tenure as president, Elder Richards instituted regular night sessions, witnessed the cessation of earlier practices such as baptism for health and administering to the sick in the temple, and led the weekly temple meeting of the prayer circle once presided over by President John Taylor. (Such prayer circle organizations were formally disbanded in 1978.)

In 1937 Elder Richards was released as temple president and sustained as acting patriarch to the Church, filling a vacancy that had lasted more than five years. Elder Richards provided that service for five years. His sons, George F., Jr., and Joel, became stake patriarchs. His son LeGrand served four missions, was bishop of three wards, president of a stake, and presiding bishop from 1938 until his call to the Council of the Twelve in 1952.

One of the most appealing characteristics of George F. Richards was the close love he manifested towards his family. George F., Jr., remembered when his father, nearing ninety,

114

put an arm around him and said, "Son, it almost seems that we have grown up as boys together."

This warmth extended to others as well. When one of the authors was an Aaronic Priesthood quorum president, Elder Richards called him out of the congregation to speak at stake conference, placed his hand on the boy's shoulder, and said, "The future of the Church rests with stalwart young brethren like this."

Elder George F. Richards died in 1950. When he was born, eighty thousand Latter-day Saints resided in four stakes and seven missions. When he died, more than a million Saints lived in one hundred eighty stakes and forty-three missions. During the forty-four years of his apostleship, Church membership had tripled. Improved priesthood and auxiliary programs, expansion of the missionary force, temple-building, and other developments were part of his experience as a General Authority. In him the dedicated Richards family had a strong link in generations of devoted service.

Chapter 13

Helen Sekaquaptewa: Traditions of the Fathers

"Oraibi" is the name of an ancient Hopi village in northeastern Arizona. Strategically located at the end of a mesa, Oraibi is protected on three sides by steep, rocky cliffs. It has been inhabited continuously for five centuries. In 1890 Oraibi was divided into two factions: traditionalists (called Hostiles), who opposed white man's ways, and progressives (called Friendlies), who favored accommodation.

In 1898 an Oraibi traditionalist woman, Sehynim, gave birth to her third child, a daughter named "Dowawisnima" (dew-wow-iss-nima), which means a "trail marked by sand." Many years later, Dowawisnima recalled, that as a young child she used to watch the principal and the truant officer start out from the school below the mesa and, walk up the trail to round up the traditionalist children. Sehynim and her husband Talashongnewa hid their children, but one day Dowawisnima was caught and escorted down the mesa to the school. There she and the other traditionalist children were bathed, dressed in white man's clothes, and given white man's names. Dowawisnima became "Helen."

The parents who voluntarily entered their children into school were given an ax, a hoe, a shovel, and a rake to farm

their lands. But the traditionalists spurned modern implements, preferring their homemade tools of wood and stone.
When Helen returned from school each day, her mother took
off "the clothes of the detested white man," and, like the other
traditionalist parents, warned, "Don't take the pencil in your
hand. If you do, it means you give consent to what they want
you to do. Don't do it."

Helen rather liked the school. It was warm inside, and the
clothes were comfortable. But the children of the progressives
began to tease Helen and the others, calling them "Hostiles,"
and refusing to play with them. Occasionally, "the Friendly
children ran ahead up the trail and gathered rocks and threw
them down at us. When I learned that the kids were 'hostile' to
us, I didn't want to go to school."

Tensions between the two sides mounted. When Helen was
seven, the progressives physically drove the traditionalists
from their homes. The federal government tried to reconcile
the two camps, but the traditionalists insisted that the chief
who had departed from the Hopi way must be beheaded. The
government superintendent declined that proposition but was
unable to find an acceptable alternative.

Winter was approaching, but rather than risk bloodshed,
the traditionalists, actually a majority, moved five miles away
to Hotevilla springs. There was no time to quarry sandstone to
build a pueblo, so the men cut down cedar trees and built
Navajo-type hogans. Within a few weeks, forty to fifty domed
hogans were ready. But the Hopis were not accustomed to the
Navajo method of cooking over an open fire in the center of the
home, and for a time something caught fire nearly every day.

Soon federal troops arrived. Seventy-five fathers were
arrested and, with their eighty-two school age children, taken
forty miles away to Keams Canyon. Seven old men, a handful
of younger ones who promised to cooperate, twenty-three
preschool children, and sixty-three women were all that
remained.

At Keams Canyon the men were sentenced to ninety days of
hard labor. The children were taken to a government boarding
school. It was night when they arrived, and Helen was

117

bewildered by the electric lights. "I had never seen so much light at night. I was all mixed up and thought it was daytime." Again their Hopi clothes were taken and they were dressed in white man's clothes. "We got real homesick," Helen recalled. "Evenings we would gather in a corner and cry softly so the matron would not hear and scold or spank us. . . . We didn't understand a word of English and didn't know what to say or do. . . . At night when the doors were closed and locked . . . [some of the progressive girls] would take our native clothes from the boxes and put them on and dance around making fun of us."

One morning Helen heard the clinking sounds of a chain gang coming down the road. She and the other children ran to the wire fence surrounding the compound. There came the Hotevilla fathers on their way to build a canyon road. Chained together in two's, they had difficulty walking but did not appear ashamed "because they knew in their hearts they had done no wrong." A guard prevented the fathers from stopping to talk with their children, but every morning the children ran to the fence to wait for their fathers. "We would cry if we saw them and cry if we didn't." Helen saw her father only once before he and several other leaders were sent to prison at Fort Huachuca for a year.

Back at Hotevilla, without the men and older children, life was lonely and the hardships severe. The corn baskets were soon empty and survival everyone's preoccupation. With only a mule for transportation, Helen's mother was able to visit her daughter only once.

At the end of the school year, progressive parents came in wagons, on horseback, and on burros to take their children home. Traditional parents would not promise to bring their children back in September, so they remained virtual prisoners in the boarding school.

In September 1907 Helen watched as government wagons descended the canyon road her father had helped build. When the wagon train reached the campground, out came the prisoners of Fort Huachuca. Helen spotted her father. "He was dressed in an old military uniform and looked fine and young

118

and straight to me, and I was proud of him." Talashongnewa visited overnight with Helen and then hurried home on foot to Hotevilla.

After four years at the Keams Canyon school, Talashongnewa and the other traditionalist fathers obtained permission to take their children home for two weeks. It was a joyful caravan of fifty boys and girls, each riding a burro with their fathers walking alongside, that made the forty-mile journey to Hotevilla. Finally Helen lived in the traditional Hopi stone houses the fathers had built to replace the hogans. When September came, the children did not return to school. Instead, Helen spent the year, "learning from my mother the things a Hopi girl should know."

But the following year, the soldiers came again and loaded them into the wagons for Keams Canyon. The school had a new superintendent. "If I had my way you would never see your homes again," he told them. "You would live like white people."

Nevertheless, Helen made the most of her opportunities. She earned money running the post laundry during the summer and occasionally worked in the homes of government employees. But more important, Helen learned. She enjoyed learning. "I was a good reader and got good grades. The teachers favored me and whenever visitors came they always called on me to recite. I was not the most popular girl and my ability did not help me socially, it only made the others jealous."

In 1915 Helen completed the sixth grade and wanted to continue her education elsewhere. She and a friend were permitted to go home on condition that they would return in two weeks. "We will humor our parents," they decided. "We will do what they want; dress in Hopi traditional clothes; let them fix our hair in whorls while we are there, anything to please them." Anything to get their permission to go on to the Indian school at Phoenix. Apparently successful, the girls returned to Keams Canyon in ten days and soon were on their way to Phoenix.

Discipline at the Phoenix Indian School was "military

style," the most unruly being whipped with a harness strap. Runaway girls were set to work "cleaning the yards, even cutting grass with scissors, while wearing a card that said, 'I ran away.' Boys were put in the school jail. . . . Repeaters had their heads shaved and had to wear a dress to school."

Helen saw injustice and cruelty all around her. She vowed she would never be unkind to others but would help whenever she could. "If someone does you wrong," her father had taught, "do not try to pay him back and get revenge; rather, be humble and feel in your heart, 'Some day I will do something good for that person, and do it.' " She also remembered his saying, "Anytime you have more than others—more blessings— you should share. Whenever you see other people suffering want, if you have something, give them some."

In Phoenix, Helen met Emory Sekaquaptewa, whose story paralleled hers in many ways. "I had always been a wallflower, and Emory was the best looking (and the best) boy in school. When we would read the story of the ugly duckling in our school reader, I always thought of myself as the ugly duckling. Now it was like the story; I felt like a beautiful swan."

When she graduated from high school, Helen returned home after what had amounted to a thirteen-year absence. But she was no longer a traditionalist. She refused to wear the traditional costumes her brother had woven especially for her. Instead, she gave them to her older sister Verlie. Verlie had no sympathy for Helen's new ways of thinking, but their mother was so happy to have Helen back, she no longer insisted that Helen follow the traditions.

Soon after her return, Helen met Sarah Abbott, a middle-aged nurse who had learned the Hopi language and traveled on foot and on horseback to visit the sick throughout the reservation. They became close friends; and whenever Helen felt the tension was too great at home, she went to Miss Abbott's.

In the fall of 1918 an influenza epidemic swept through the reservation. Helen was among the few who escaped serious illness, but her mother and a brother died. Because she was unmarried and living at home, Helen felt it was her duty to

120

make a home for her father and younger brothers, but Verlie moved her family in, and Helen went to work for Miss Abbott. She fed babies, chopped firewood, and cooked cornmeal mush for the sick.

At home the pressure intensified—Helen took too many baths, she washed her clothes too often, she read books. Emory was needed at his home to care for sick relatives, and Helen was lonely.

Finally, after several weeks, Emory visited Helen again. Their common experiences during the epidemic had brought them even closer together, and they decided to be married.

Hoping that a traditional ceremony would improve feelings in the family, Helen and Emory arranged for the elaborate Hopi ritual. First came a pre-dawn washing of their hair, then the twisting together of a strand from each "as a symbol of acceptance of the new in-law into the clan and also to bind the marriage contract as they said, 'Now you are united never to go apart.'" Then, their hair still wet, Emory and Helen walked to the eastern edge of the village and prayed in silence "for a good life together, for children, and to be together all of our lives and never stray from each other."

That same morning, Emory's father distributed cotton throughout the village, where it was cleaned in one day. Over the next few nights the men carded it, and in one day spun it into thread and wove it into one large robe, one small robe, and a long girdle to be tied around the waist. (Later, as part of the ceremony, the bride's father would thank the men for making the apparel that would "make his daughter eligible to enter the world of the hereafter.")

As the days of ritual continued, Emory and Helen were troubled. They wanted to be married "legally" as well. So they made arrangements for a Mennonite service. But with inner harmony came outer discord. Helen's family was so upset, that she went to the home of one of her school teachers to dress for the service. Symbolically, the white dress, like her Hopi dress, was handmade. Helen had earned the money, bought the material, and sewed every stitch herself. It had won second prize in the state fair, and Helen had worn it only once before

121

her wedding.

In February 1919 Helen and Emory were married by a Mennonite missionary. Then they returned to Emory's village to complete the Hopi ceremony. In accordance with traditionalist custom, the couple lived with the bride's family for a time. But the tension proved too great and they soon struck out on their own for Idaho.

Idaho was cold and the winter quickly consumed their savings. In 1920 they returned to Hotevilla, bought a wagon and four horses, and started freighting supplies from Winslow and Flagstaff to Oraibi. Emory also farmed on clan land twelve miles southwest of Hotevilla and worked on government construction projects in Keams Canyon.

At first they seemed alien to the traditionalist community at Hotevilla.

> Our lives were a combination of what we thought was the good of both cultures, the Hopi way and what we had learned at school. Whenever we departed from the traditions, our neighbors would scorn us. They were greatly offended because we were friendly with the government workers, the teachers, and the nurses, and even let them come into our house. When I washed my clothes and hung them out to dry or worked in my little garden plot, I could feel critical eyes following my every move. When I went to the spring for water, nearly every time I would meet a woman on the trail or at the spring who would bawl me out about something; even the clothes I wore on my back were taboo. I didn't wear the traditional dress. I did not enter wholeheartedly into all of the community social and religious events. Good traditional Hopi women sit all day in the plaza, maybe several days at a time, watching the dances. They have so many that I begrudged the time. I would rather stay home and care for my house, or read, which I often did. I was aware that my neighbors were talking about me, mimicking, and generally belittling me all the time.

When a serious skin disease infected the village, Helen and Emory voluntarily accepted the treatment, bathing in a treated solution provided by the government. But most Hotevilla residents refused. Because the infection could not be eradicated unless everyone cooperated, the health department was prepared to enforce compliance. Emory went to Keams

122

Canyon and brought back large steel water troughs. One was put on one side of the school house for the men and the other on the opposite side for the women. The traditionalists gathered at the chief's home, where the police rounded them up and drove them to the schoolhouse. "A few women would not budge," Helen recalled, "so the police picked them up one by one screaming and kicking and ducked the women, clothes and all, with much splashing and shouting."

Following the dip, many sat down in the sand and defiantly rubbed dirt all over their bodies. One woman stopped at Helen's house on her way home and shouted, "Take your children and get out. Go and live with the white people." The resentment was deep, but Helen and Emory refused to abandon their people or their principles. They remained, not to fight, but to convert. "Destroy your enemy by making him your friend," they decided.

And it worked. Over the years, with repeated acts of kindness and concern, they won over many former enemies. In 1953 the Hopi Tribal Council nominated Emory as a tribal judge. Approved by the government superintendent, he commuted to Keams Canyon twice a week to help administer justice among his people. In spite of animosity between the tribes, Helen and Emory adopted a Navajo boy and later another boy and a Hopi girl. Helen reared them with the eight of her own ten children who survived infancy.

Once, when a group of Mormons passed through Hotevilla, Helen went to hear the sermon. She remembered hearing some of the older people talk about the Mormon "Jee-co-ba," as they called Jacob Hamblin, and listened with interest. But the first full-time missionaries did not come until 1951. When they heard that Helen's oldest son was thinking of going to BYU, they encouraged him so persuasively that he left right away. "What they taught sounded good to me," Helen said, "like a familiar philosophy, like the teachings we were used to, like the Hopi way." The Book of Mormon "sounded like a familiar story." The Bible and Book of Mormon "helped us to understand the Hopi traditions, and the Hopi traditions help us to understand these books of scripture. . . . I was really converted the first week and believed everything, although I was not baptized right soon." Feeling sorry when her neighbors closed their doors to the missionaries, Helen invited the missionaries to come to her home whenever they felt lonesome, homesick or sad.

Ironically, it was Helen's father, stubbornly opposed to white culture, who was the unwitting agent preparing his daughter's family for Mormonism. During the longer winter evenings he recited, over and over, "the teachings of the kiva." He acknowledged that oral transmission had created some inaccuracies but, as Helen recalled, he insisted that "the written record will be brought to the Hopis by the white man. There will be many religions taught. You will need to be wise to recognize and choose the right church. It will teach you to be humble and will not try to force you into it. When that time comes we should all forsake our native religion and join this true church."

Helen's son Wayne joined the church in Phoenix and baptized his mother, a brother and a sister there in 1953. Helen moved to Phoenix in 1954 to be with her five children who were attending the Phoenix Indian School. Emory took care of the ranch, worked in the Oraibi trading post and attended to his judicial responsibilities. Helen spent six winters in Phoenix until the children completed their schooling and then returned to Hotevilla.

Called to be district Relief Society president, Helen routinely walked the twelve miles from the ranch to Hotevilla, slept over night, and then hitchhiked into Holbrook for district meetings. She tried to attend every Relief Society meeting in her district, even though it meant long walks to do so. "If I'm not there," she explained, "some of them don't hold meetings."

When Emory began complaining about the time she spent away from home, Helen thought that perhaps she should resign her Church calling. "I thought about it all day long and toward evening I just couldn't do it. I had dedicated myself to this work." She said nothing to Emory during dinner and went to bed. Soon she heard someone open the screen door, walk

124

across the floor, and sit on her. She was terrified. She could not scream or struggle. Mentally she commanded, "Get behind me, Satan, in the name of Jesus Christ." The intruder "stepped right down and walked out the same way he came in." Shaken, Helen lay in her sweat-soaked bed through the night.

In the morning she told Emory what had happened. He grumbled that he hadn't heard anything, but "from then on he started to soften his heart. He started to come to church with me." Emory never did join the Church, but he participated in meetings and spoke and prayed when invited.

Desiring to be both a good Mormon and a good Hopi, Helen routinely visits the homes of her many friends and neighbors, whether they are members of the Church or not. She watches for signs that food or clothing is needed, respectfully visits the aged and, when needed, quietly does their laundry.

Such acts of Christian service have enhanced the reputation of the Church in northeastern Arizona. In recent years it has grown slowly but steadily. Through the united efforts of the Navajo and Hopi Saints, the Moencopi Chapel was erected at Tuba City and dedicated in January 1965 by Elder Spencer W. Kimball. In 1974 the branch became a ward, part of the Page Arizona Stake.

"When I think upon my children and the kind of people that they are," Helen reflects, "a feeling of joy and pride fills my heart, and I say to myself, I have had a good life. . . . My childhood, my school days, and marriage, those years were only laying the foundation for wifehood and motherhood—the best years of my life, the real living."

Perhaps this intense devotion to family was Helen's quiet triumph in her quest to unite Hopi ways and a traditionally white church. She married Hopi family pride to the Mormon doctrine of family exaltation. Despite his years of opposition to Helen's choices, her father finally admitted, "You are a good daughter. You have good children. I marvel at the way you stood up against people. . . . And we all lived better because of it."

Chapter 14

Ephraim and Edna Ericksen: The Philosopher and the Trail Builder

Ephraim Ericksen characterized his father, Bendt Jensen Ericksen as "one of thousands who made Brigham Young great." Converted in Denmark in 1851, Bendt remained in his homeland as a missionary and Church leader for twelve years before emigrating to Utah. He was alone. His wife Hilda and their three children had died in an epidemic. When he arrived in the Salt Lake Valley, Brigham Young sent Bendt and his new wife, Anna Jurtsen, to colonize Milton, Idaho. Until their home was finished, they lived in a dugout, a cave in the bank of the Bear River—which no doubt contributed to Anna's premature death. Later, Bendt and two new wives, Ellen Jonasson and Sophia Jensen, pioneered Bear River City northwest of Brigham City. While Bendt fulfilled two missions to Denmark and one to the Navajos, Ellen and Sophia raised children and eked out a meagre existence. Bendt married Anna Sophia Danielsen in 1878 and she persuaded him to move to Logan, where her second child, Ephraim, was born on 2 January 1882.

Not long after Ephraim's birth, Bendt moved two of his

three wives and their seven children a few miles north to Preston, Idaho, where they all lived in a one-room cabin. Even by pioneer standards the Ericksens were poor. Bread and milk was the customary evening meal. Danes were on the bottom of the social ladder in the Mormon communities of southern Idaho, and despite Bendt's record of Church service, he and his family were still "Danish"—a term of derision in some quarters.

Ephraim was twelve when his father died. To help support his mother, older sister, and younger brother, he worked on the family farm, on railroad construction, and on the Mink Creek canal. As a result, he was able to attend school only three or four months a year. At the age of twenty-one he graduated from the Oneida Stake Academy and with his brother Alma, left Preston to attend the Brigham Young College in Logan, where their mother soon joined them.

Ephraim worked as a school janitor to pay his tuition. He had only one change of clothes, but his genial manner attracted many friends, and he was elected student body president. His pugilistic skills also won respect.

Ephraim's most influential teachers at the BYC were Mosiah Hall, who had studied with John Dewey and led Ephraim into critical biblical scholarship, and William H. Chamberlin, who taught Ephraim the philosophy known as "personal idealism." Chamberlin had a profound impact on the young farmboy. Personal idealism "impressed me as having great religious significance since it advocated the ultimate reality of human personality.... [It] struck me as just another way of saying, The soul of man is eternal," Ephraim recalled. To him it was Mormon doctrine in philosophical garb, and when B.H. Roberts challenged the BYC students to answer the attacks of non-Mormon scholars, Ephraim decided he could best serve his Church and his people by becoming a philosopher.

While attending the BYC, Ephraim met and fell in love with Edna Clark, daughter of Hyrum D. and Ann Eliza Porter Clark. Edna's background was quite different from Ephraim's. The Clark and the Porter families both traced their Church participation to Nauvoo and even earlier. Edna's father and grandfather were successful ranchers and prominent church-men in Star Valley, Wyoming, and Farmington, Utah. Attractive, and a talented singer, Edna enjoyed the attentions of numerous suitors.

Ephraim was poor, rather shabbily dressed, moved awk-wardly on the dance floor, and "couldn't carry a tune in a bucket." But Edna was impressed by the way he treated his mother, his personal integrity, and his idealism. She was sorry to see him leave in 1908 for the University of Chicago.

Traveling east by train, Ephraim and Alma stopped at Independence, Missouri, where they met Joseph Smith III. "He was then quiet and old—friendly, but not particularly impressive. But we had the satisfaction of having seen the son of the Prophet." They also visited their uncle William G. Danielsen, a former Utah blacksmith who dreamed he had been called to start a plow factory in Jackson County preparatory to the return of the Saints. He persuaded President Joseph F. Smith to help finance the enterprise with Church funds and got into production. Poor management later led to financial difficulties, the Church eventually withdrew its support, and the project failed. "Uncle Bill's dream apparently did not come from Heaven, but from his own head," Ephraim concluded.

When Ephraim and Alma arrived in Chicago they had less than ten dollars between them. However, both were soon granted scholarships and began their studies—Alma in law, and Ephraim in philosophy.

The University of Chicago was a center of pragmatic philosophy, social and religious psychology, liberal theology, social gospel, and naturalistic religion. After his first year Ephraim decided that philosophy had not destroyed his basic religious convictions, but "I was ready to give up some of the traditional beliefs about miracles . . . and that there was only one true church . . . , but I continued to believe in the existence of God . . . , that He loved human beings everywhere and that the sincere efforts of persons and of organized groups to advance the truth, the beautiful, and the just, expresses God's

128

will. This was Chamberlin's philosophy, and to me it was Mormonism at its best."

But to Horace H. Cummings, superintendent of the Church school system, it was not Mormonism of any kind. He informed Ephraim that the philosophy he was being taught was not the kind that was wanted by the Church. Because Ephraim hoped to return to Utah and teach in the Church schools, he took the superintendent's advice and transferred into economics—still "holding fast to my philosophy," for "it appeared to me . . . that a man of Mr. Cummings's type may not continue as head of the system, and that the attitude of the Church toward science and philosophy may change."

In 1910 Ephraim returned to Utah and married Edna Clark in the Salt Lake Temple. In the summer they began gathering material for what was to become Ephraim's dissertation on Mormon history. University of Utah President John A. Widtsoe and Elder Joseph Fielding Smith, the Church Historian, gave encouragement and help in locating documents and eyewitnesses of historical events.

The next year Ephraim was named principal of the Church's Murdock Academy in Beaver, Utah. When he and Edna arrived, they found the academy housed in abandoned Fort Cameron, a short distance from town.

Boxes of books and clothing stood unopened on the Ericksens' living room floor on the morning the census examiner appeared at the door. Emphasizing the need for accuracy, he thoroughly questioned Edna about her husband's vital statistics. Then he took out another questionnaire and asked her name and occupation. Proudly she answered, "I am a homemaker and a mother." "Nothing," he wrote. Edna immediately became a "feminist."

At Murdock, Ephraim was principal, teacher, fund-raiser, branch counselor, and athletic coach; Edna was counselor in the branch Relief Society, assistant dean of students, substitute mother, nursemaid, midwife, and the lead in several school operettas.

Ephraim was a popular but outspoken principal. On three occasions he was reprimanded by stake and General Authorities for "attempting to make the school more important than the whole Church." At one stake conference, he preached on "the eternal glory of education" and "the sacred mission of the Murdock Academy." He urged the boys to finish high school so they could proselytize effectively anywhere—even on university campuses. When he finished, Elder Joseph W. McMurrin of the First Council of Seventy arose and cautioned that what was needed was a strong testimony, not secular knowledge. Undaunted, the self-appointed apostle of education continued to proclaim his gospel throughout the region. "I know the Gospel is true," he said, "insofar as it is interpreted correctly." The "correct" interpretation was "faith, charity, and education. These three, and greatest of these is education."

In the spring of 1914 Ephraim took a short leave of absence to complete his Ph.D. course work at Chicago, returning in time for his annual student recruitment drive throughout the southwest quadrant of the state. In the spring of 1915 he accepted a position at the University of Utah—assistant professor of philosophy at $1700 a year.

In 1918 Ephraim finished his dissertation, a critical study of Mormon group life. Though it was highly praised in the *London Times* and various periodicals, *The Psychological and Ethical Aspects of Mormon Group Life* was not well received in Utah. Ephraim was told that Dr. Widtsoe found it "historically and scientifically unsound" and that it had been on sale for only a few hours at the Deseret Bookstore before it was quickly boxed up and returned to the publisher.

Ephraim's interpretation of Mormon history was not what Latter-day Saints were accustomed to. He suggested that Joseph Smith "received his inspiration from the group and in turn reflected its life in such a way as to give it restimulation." He praised Joseph Smith's sensitivity to the spiritual needs of his people and Brigham Young's pragmatic genius in overcoming the challenges of the Great Basin and founding a state. But he was critical of the Church's hostility towards the biological sciences and biblical scholarship, and its close alignment with capitalism. "There is a growing tendency to take sides with the capitalistic class and with large corporations

130

against the laboring classes," he charged. "The philosophy of the church leaders was at one time radical and socialistic; it is now conservative and capitalistic. . . . The United Order is as far from their minds as is socialism from the minds of the owners of large corporations."

"What Mormonism needs today," he wrote, "is the vitalization of its institutions, which need to be put into use rather than merely contemplated. . . . When Mormonism finds more glory in working out new social ideals than in the contemplating of past achievements or the beauty of its own theological system, it will begin to feel its old-time strength."

Despite this strident critique, the Church soon gave Ephraim an opportunity to help "vitalize its institutions" and "work out new social programs." In 1922, the same year his dissertation was published, he was called to the general board of the Young Men's Mutual Improvement Association.

Edna had received a similar calling two years before—to the Primary General Board. A much lower percentage of boys than girls was attending Primary, and the general board decided that a special committee should be assigned to the problem. When the names of the committee members were read to the board, Edna's name was not on the list. She was disappointed; after all, she was the only board member with three Primary-age boys. Then Primary President Louie B. Felt asked Edna to see her in her office. Edna called home to have the boys put the potatoes in the oven and start dinner without her.

Sister Felt called Edna to chair the new committee. Edna was not prepared for *that* much responsibility. She was especially conscious of the fact that she had never graduated from high school. But Sister Felt was certain. "She put her hands on my head," Edna recalled, "and gave me a blessing. It was quite unusual. She recognized in her prayer that it was a tremendous responsibility and promised if I would be faithful and diligent, the way would be opened." Sister Felt emphasized that Edna's husband and children would be her best resource.

When Edna arrived home, the family was eating dinner. She began to tell them what had happened, but overwhelmed by feelings of inadequacy, she broke down and cried. "If I just knew how to do it," she sobbed, "but I don't." She would have to drop her kindergarten training class at the university, she told them, and start reading—preparing *somehow*.

Then in prompt fulfillment of Sister Felt's blessing, Ephraim spoke up. "Edna, you will never find a better textbook than the one you have around this table." He and the boys "pledged their support to me right there. I told them I couldn't carry the whole load alone. Their support was beautiful." Ephraim devoted every Saturday afternoon to helping Edna organize and think through the problems of creating a new Church program for boys.

Some of Edna's committee felt they could get the boys to their meetings more regularly by emphasizing that attendance was a commandment. "But Ephraim and I had the feeling that we should start where the child was, and build from there. We had to know who the children were and what interested them first. . . . So we instructed the ward primaries to get acquainted with the boys and find out what they enjoyed, where their interests were."

The Church's Boy Scout leader Oscar A. Kirkham suggested the name "Trail Builder" and Edna's committee developed the program. At first it was just the Trekkers and Guides (ages 9 and 10). Two years later the Blazers were added. The committee searched for a way of recognizing achievement and Edna suggested the bandalo with felt badges. Thus, the Trail Builder program began—a program that endured without major revision for fifty years and was used as a model in developing the Cub Scouts of America.

Edna continued to chair the committee overseeing Trail Builder work until her release in 1940. During her twenty years on the Primary board, she also wrote many articles for the *Children's Friend*, and in addition to her Church assignments she sang in the Tabernacle Choir and appeared as guest soloist in the old Salt Lake Theatre, on KSL radio, and with the Grieg Male Chorus.

Ephraim was just as diligent in his Church calling. Soon after his appointment to the YMMIA board, he was appointed chairman of the new Young Men's and Young Women's recreation committee. The committee previewed motion pictures for Church events, and published "Standards for Social Dancing." ("Jazz in orchestra dance playing might be defined as 'departure from the correct,' making the instruments perform that which is not written, and in a way contrary to their accepted, proper use. This type of playing is rank, 'faking,' and should not be tolerated by intelligent people.")

But a more enduring contribution was the establishment of cultural and recreational MIA festivals. By 1926 virtually every stake and ward sponsored festivals in dozens of categories, including poetry and essay writing, vocal quartets and choruses, orchestra, band, drama, ballroom dancing, folk dancing, instrumental and vocal solos, fife and drum, debate, retold story, declamation, field and track, "van ball," and basketball. Winners on regional levels came to Salt Lake City to participate in Churchwide competitions.

In 1931 Ephraim was released as chairman of the recreation committee to develop an MIA program for young adults twenty-four to thirty-five. With Elsie Talmage Brandley, Ephraim wrote the first manual, *Challenging Problems of the Twentieth Century*. Published in the midst of the Depression, the topics were relevant and controversial: "The Economic Challenge," "Challenges to the Family," "Recreation and the New Challenge to Leadership," "Religion: Its Intellectual and Social Changes."

Harking back to themes he had emphasized in *Mormon Group Life*, Ephraim portrayed science and philosophy as "loyal friends" of religion. Frequent positive allusions to articles by non-Mormon social scientists encouraged MIA members to look beyond Mormonism, as well as within, for social direction.

Study questions at the end of each chapter were not designed for easy answers: "What are some of the new intellectual achievements that impose a reconstruction on traditional religious thought? Does religion have the responsibility to settle questions of scientific and intellectual character? What is more nearly the function of religion (a) to conserve inherited beliefs, (b) to promote new and more adequate scientific ideas, (c) to employ new scientific and philosophical ideas in the interest of finer faith and more abundant living?"

The experimental year was a popular success, and the manual was expanded for the following year to include trends in education, unemployment, community health, family life, leisure time, isolationism in foreign policy, social justice, and capitalism. Another manual, "Social Changes and Spiritual Values," was authorized for 1933. A study indicated that attendance in the new department had risen dramatically, with only three of twenty-nine participating stakes reporting negative reactions.

But in April 1933 Elder John A. Widtsoe, just back from presiding over the European missions, spoke to the board. According to the minutes of the meeting he "commented on the abundance of material contained in many of the manuals and said that much of it was beyond his comprehension. . . . He further stated that unless we flavor all we do and all we have with the message of the Prophet Joseph Smith, we are far afield, adding, 'If this organization intends to give extension courses like the University of Utah, we are missing our purpose.' "

YMMIA Superintendent George Albert Smith immediately appointed a committee to reexamine the goals of MIA. Under Elder Widtsoe's direction the committee recommended the new theme of MIA be "to help make real Latter-day Saints," and that an editorial committee be appointed to edit and correlate all manuscripts for study courses, programs, and activity outlines. Ephraim and one other board member voiced strenuous objections but they were overruled, the board was dissolved, and a new board appointed without the "progressives."

In the meantime, Edna had become active in various civic organizations—in addition to raising four sons and a daughter, and developing the Trail Builder program. In 1932 she became chairman of the American Home Division of the State Federation of Women's Clubs and state chairman of the Better Homes Organization. She also led the singing at Democratic conventions and rallies. One day in 1933 a party organizer came to ask Ephraim if he would consider running for the Utah House of Representatives. He had been an outspoken proponent of the labor movement and was considered a good prospect for political office. But Edna knew he was too preoccupied with the MIA manuals and his responsibilities as professor at the University to run. Half-jokingly she suggested someday she might run. The organizer took her seriously. Ephraim seconded the idea, and within a few weeks Edna was sitting at desk 42 in the Utah's House of Representatives.

In the House she worked for equal pay for women, the rights of midwives, and other health and educational causes. She served in the House until 1935, and in the State Senate from 1941 to 1947. Among her achievements in the Senate was the appointment of Maude May Babcock as senate chaplain, the first woman chaplain of a state legislature in the United States. Edna also chaired the committee that commissioned the Brigham Young statue for the United States Capitol Building. She presided at the Washington unveiling in 1950, thus becoming, Ephraim joked, "the only woman to put Brigham in his place."

After his release from the YMMIA board, Ephraim taught the high priests group in the University Ward, served as president of the Western Division of the American Philosophical Association, and completed his book *Social Ethics* (Doubleday, 1937). In 1948, after thirty-four years, he retired from the University of Utah—only to teach at the University of Nevada from 1949 to 1952. While in Reno, Edna helped promote the first chapter of the League of Women Voters in Nevada.

Returning to Salt Lake City, Ephraim and Edna remained involved in the University Ward. Though his individual views precluded Ephraim from official callings, he attended priesthood meetings "and with proper humiliation and faith give the brethren a bit of true Christian philosophy. In the same spirit they listen attentively, yet prefer to 'remain on the Lord's side.' " The ward teachers visited monthly "and in the kindest spirit of the gospel provide me with insight into the deepest theology of Mormonism. To all of this I listen and return to

[them] measure for measure my own FOOLosophy."

Though he goodnaturedly joked about his relationship with the Church, Ephraim remained devoted to its welfare. His critique remained essentially the same as his 1918 dissertation. In 1957 he wrote, "The Mormon community has priests by the hundreds of thousands, but few prophets; and with few exceptions their prophets have been more priestly in their philosophy than prophetic."

Yet he remained optimistic. "The Priest and the Prophet will always be with us, the one to advance the Promising New and the other to defend the Hallowed Old . . . . Creative thought in Mormonism is not going to be depressed."

After a fall that confined him to a wheelchair, Edna cared for Ephraim for the last fifteen years of his life. When he passed away in 1967, she resumed her civic career, serving as receptionist for the State House and Senate, on the state Textbook and Curriculum Commission, and as a charter member of the Foster Grandparent Association.

In 1965 the University of Utah established the E.E. Ericksen Chair of Philosophy. In the contributions of his many students, friends, and associates, Ephraim's legacy continues to vibrate within the Church.

Chapter 15

Margrit Feh Lohner:
Swiss Immigrant

Louise Gammenthaler had to leave the dance early to prepare her Sunday School lesson for the next day. Edward Feh walked her home, puzzled about Louise's religious affiliation. Was she Protestant? Catholic? Finally, in desperation he asked, "Mormon?" "Well, I'm a member of The Church of Jesus Christ of Latter-day Saints." Relieved, Edward responded, "Oh, that's a beautiful name. Can I see you Sunday by the lake?"

By Sunday Edward had learned the connection between the Mormons and the Latter-day Saints. He arrived with a stack of anti-Mormon pamphlets. But Louise was also prepared—with a testimony—and challenged him to investigate. For three months Edward followed the missionaries around, hoping to find one breaking the Word of Wisdom or walking with a girl. Finally conceding defeat, he began a serious study of the gospel. Edward and Louise were married after his baptism, and Margrit, born 20 May 1914, was their only child.

The Fehs lived on the third floor of the Zurich home where Edward had been born. There was an etching studio on the first floor, Margrit's uncle lived on the second floor, and above them, on the fourth floor lived another uncle. When Margrit was about fourteen, at the beginning of the Great Depression, the Fehs obtained visas to immigrate to the United States, but

European Mission President John A. Widtsoe told Edward he was needed in Switzerland, and they stayed.

Edward became mission Sunday School superintendent, district president, and branch president, while Louise was equally involved in the auxiliaries. Thus Church activity came naturally to their ebullient daughter. Even more important, perhaps, was the confidence they instilled in her "that I was on the right track," even though Margrit was the only Latter-day Saint in her school.

President Heber J. Grant and Elders Joseph Fielding Smith, James E. Talmage, John A. Widtsoe, and Joseph F. Merrill visited their home, Elder Talmage making a special trip of several hours to give Louise a blessing when she became ill.

Once, Louise and Edward left Margrit with another Latter-day Saint family while they went on a weekend assignment and vacation. Margrit developed an ear infection early in the evening and cried for her parents all night as the family walked the floor with her.

Edward was speaking in district conference when he felt an inner voice prompting him to go home. He cut his talk short, informed the presiding officer he would be leaving, and beckoned to Louise, who was sitting in the audience. She was stunned. A vacation was a rare experience; they had hotel reservations and a full day of sightseeing scheduled. "No," he said, "we're going home."

"To me that was the most inspirational thing," Margrit recalled, "to *realize* that I needed them and they knew I needed them and came home. It's as simple as that."

Margrit was a diligent student. She was excused from her school's religion classes, however, when she proved all too willing to challenge the teacher's interpretations of scripture. Margrit had a special talent for languages, eventually becoming fluent in German, French, Dutch, Italian, and English.

Edward and Louise both sang in choirs, and Margrit remembered her mother often sang "Let the Mountains Shout for Joy" as she did the housework. They provided piano lessons for Margrit, but she had to walk twenty minutes in the

138

snow to practice in the unheated parlor of a friend's home. Ironically, Margrit resented the lessons she had pleaded for, and remembered "sitting at the piano with tears streaming down my face" through the hours of practice required by her mother. "Now [music] is my life. But it had to be drummed in when I was a teenager."

The Saturday evenings before district conferences were devoted to MIA activities, and Margrit was given "a free hand" to produce many of them, including an elaborate presentation of *Sleeping Beauty*, which called for a paper rose covering for the stage curtain. She recruited the Relief Society to make the roses, but materials still amounted to two hundred francs (about $200), and the Mutual, taken back by the magnitude of the ambitious project, fasted for an audience large enough to make it a success. But "by the time the evening arrived, we prayed that no one else would come, because they were sitting on the radiators and the window sills and everything."

Growing up in Zurich also gave Margrit the opportunity to teach Sunday School and MIA and to serve as branch organist. The Feh home also became a center for missionaries, "and I never opened a Christmas present but that it wasn't in the presence of our missionaries."

Of the native Swiss members, none became more important to Margrit than Werner A. Lohner, who was five years older than she. As a Boy Scout, he had come to help Margrit's mother polish silverware and to carry coal up from the basement. In one MIA production, Werner played the hero who was to rush in and save Margrit from the menacing Indian, Lowell Bennion (then district president and later director of the University of Utah Institute). Lowell "came closer and closer, and finally he backed me up against the wall and the hero didn't arrive—he couldn't get his boots on."

But when Werner returned from a mission to Germany, the hero had no trouble "getting his boots on." Werner claimed he had resolved to marry Margrit when she was still a child. But they were twenty-eight and twenty-three respectively when they were married on 7 May 1937. It was the civil ceremony required by Swiss law, followed by a leisurely lunch at a

lakeside hotel. In the evening the MIA sponsored the traditional Church wedding party: the mission president married
the couple again, followed by a program of readings, a
performance by the orchestra, and dancing.

Margrit's parents and Werner's mother accompanied the
newlyweds on their three-day honeymoon. Neither bride nor
groom seemed to mind the parental presence. "They really
took in all our happiness," Margrit remembered. Then, unable
to coordinate their work schedules, they took separate
vacations—Werner to his former mission field and Margrit, a
month later, to Paris and Belgium with her father.

The following year, 1938, Louise Feh fulfilled her lifelong
dream of visiting Salt Lake City and going to the temple.
Louise enjoyed herself so much she didn't want to return. She
went through the temple 153 times. But in 1939 she did return,
just as World War II erupted—which reinforced her deter-
mination to emigrate. Mission President Thomas E. McKay
accompanied them to the American consulate and recommended their visas be issued quickly. They were processed in
April 1940, and to avoid Germany and France, the family
traveled to Genoa, Italy, where they planned to sail for
America.

Margrit was worried about the war, and concerned about
the future of her twenty-month-old son and about her father's
crippling arthritis. An adverse medical report could nullify
their visas. At Genoa the ship's steward approached them,
smiled at baby Richard, and ushered them out of the waiting
room into an examination room. There they braced for
questions about Walter's arthritis. Instead, the doctor asked,

> "Where are you going?"
> "Utah."
> "Where in Utah?"
> "Salt Lake City."
> "Are you Mormons?"
> "Yes."
> "Wonderful!"
> For the first time in our lives somebody had said "Wonderful!"
> because we were Mormons. He talked about the missionaries,
> stamped our papers, and sent us into the next room.

140

Same thing:
"Where are you going?"
"Utah."
"Where in Utah."
"Salt Lake."
"Are you Mormons?"
"Yes."
"Wonderful!"
That was our introduction to the United States.

Adjustment to a new environment is difficult for most immigrants. Language differences make communication difficult and homesickness is discouraging. When they discover that the streets are not paved with gold and that they are simply members like hundreds of others instead of the center of attention in a small mission branch, many immigrants become disillusioned.

Fortunately, the Fehs and Lohners had a hundred friends waiting to greet them when they arrived in Salt Lake City. "From then on we were home, right from the first day," Margrit reported. Nevertheless, it is to her credit that she maintained a positive attitude and took advantage of every opportunity to participate in ward activities. Even while her English was still halting she accepted a call to direct a ward play, then to be the MIA activity counselor, stake music director, and in 1950, to become a member of the YWMIA General Board.

Margrit and Werner joined the Swiss Edelweiss Chorus and five years later she became its director, a position she held until 1976, when she became the organization's president. Margrit also sang in the Mormon Tabernacle Choir for seventeen years. One of her fondest memories was singing with the choir at the dedication of the Swiss Temple. It was her first trip home in fifteen years. "I cried when I touched Swiss soil."

Margrit's two daughters were born in the United States. Her father died in 1947, and her mother lived with Margrit until her death in 1965. Secure in the knowledge that things were well at home, Margrit also worked at a department store, then for the *Deseret News*, and for many years at the Genealogical Society.

Margrit's term on the YWMIA General Board was filled with exciting experiences, and her enthusiasm and organizational flair helped make them successful. "I am just a stickler for details and advance preparation," she explained. "I always have a list of what to do, what's to be done for this day, what's to be done by the end of the week, and then I cross them off and carry over what isn't done."

The excitement of the 1958 music festival production gave Margrit particularly fond memories. Crawford Gates chaired a committee which wrote "Praise Ye the Lord," which begins with the creation and ends with the hallelujahs and hosannahs of the final judgment. An international music festival followed, then a revival of *Promised Valley* that had been written for the 1947 centennial and was even translated into French and German. Also inaugurated during the 1960s were quartet festivals, Young Artists concerts, and Spring Sings.

Margrit also reported, with a little pride, that in 1970, after a year's work with the Laurel conference committee of girls on how to conduct meetings, organize, and plan, that "we never sat on the stage, we never conducted a meeting . . . and these five young girls conducted meetings just like 'pros'." And there was special satisfaction when she had only one 6:30 A.M. rehearsal to teach hymns to a chorus. Thinking optimistically, she printed 300 sheets of music, hoped for 200 singers, and was overwhelmed when 750 showed up.

For Margrit all of these activities were infused with a strong spirituality. One of her first assignments was to write a lesson about Schubert for a YWMIA manual. After reading three books, she knelt down and prayed, 'Father in Heaven, I know all about Schubert, but what do I do with it now?!' And I wrote a lesson about Schubert and about these evenings of music that Schubert had with his friends . . . that was in the manual for six years. To me that was a lesson right from the beginning that I can't do it by myself, but with the Lord's help I can."

Following her release from the general board in 1972, Margrit served eight years on the Church Music Committee, where she saw the music festivals mushroom. In 1970 there were 7,500 applications to sing in the all-Church music festival. By 1972 the number had grown to 8,500 for the Utah regional festival alone.

Yet these popular achievements, which often involved thousands of participants, were always intended to benefit individuals, a fact Margrit never forgot. She recalled with pleasure a letter from a boy in Hurricane, Utah, who applied for the music festival because "I decided to improve myself and [it was] the first thing that came along." After the festival he wrote again to thank the committee for the opportunity.

Margrit poured her energy into doing rather than into questioning and worrying. Blessed with the ability to think quickly and make decisions rapidly, she was ruefully aware that the accompanying disadvantage is impatience. She said, "I had to learn patience," but added, "I never question or argue with the General Authorities. . . . I've already taken the short-cut—to do it by obedience, rather than by experience."

With pleasure Margrit quoted "sentence sermons" learned from her co-workers: "*Nothing* but the best is good enough for the Kingdom of the Lord" (Crawford Gates), and "What should not happen should not be invited to happen" (Richard L. Evans).

Asked how she would like to be remembered, the vivacious grandmother paused briefly, then responded, "Ah, I don't know . . . I'd just like to be remembered by my family as having been industrious and thoughtful, and serving . . . and loving the Lord."

Chapter 16

T. Edgar Lyon: Missionary, Educator, Historian

T. Edgar Lyon was born in Salt Lake City in 1903, the eighth child of David and Mary Cairns Lyon. When he was eight or nine, Ed began to work after school in his father's print shop and, when he was twelve, began spending the summers with his older brother Paul at Jackson Hole, Wyoming, haying, grubbing out sagebrush, pulling down timbers and stripping the logs, and helping build Paul's log cabin.

Graduating from the Latter-day Saint High School, Ed studied for two years at the University of Utah before he was called on a mission to Holland. He was somewhat apprehensive about the mission because he had not done particularly well in Latin at high school and feared the Dutch language might prevent him from being an effective missionary. However, when Melvin J. Ballard set him apart, he blessed him with the gift of tongues and the gift of healing.

Following the blessing, Ed departed without language training or other missionary preparation. After a harrowing ocean voyage through iceberg fields, the group arrived at Liverpool, where they boarded a train for Harwich. But heavy rains had washed out the bridges and delayed their arrival. The train finally pulled up right along the quay just as the boat was leaving for Rotterdam. It was brought back and the missionaries jumped aboard, only to learn that their berths had been given to others. They spent a sleepless night on the floor of a dining hall. When they finally arrived at Rotterdam, Ed and his companions were "dead tired, hardly able to keep our eyes open," but they were immediately whisked away to church and invited to sit on the stand.

Naturally Ed could not understand the opening song or prayer. When the first speaker began to talk, Ed noticed both of his companions were fast asleep, but "I was wide awake, sitting on the end of my bench, and I was understanding everything the man said." He talked about the ancient Christian church, the apostasy and restoration. Ed was amazed. Though he knew no Dutch, he "got pretty well the whole gist of the thing."

A second speaker addressed the congregation and Ed understood his talk as well. But of the third talk "I never got a word out of it except the 'Jesus Christus, Amen' at the end." To him it was fulfillment of Elder Ballard's blessing. He was convinced that nothing but a spiritual gift could have given him the understanding of those talks.

He began studying the Dutch Book of Mormon, learning the words as he went along. One day, before he knew much of the language, he was tracting an old section of town. It was not unusual in his mission for companions to split up and work different sides of the street, and Ed was alone. He met a Dutchman "about six foot six inches I guess, with broad shoulders. . . . He was raking the leaves up and had a little fire burning." The man refused Ed's tract. Ed persisted. Again the man refused, then took the pamphlet and threw it into the fire. "I walked away and something turned me around and I went back and I said, 'Mijn Heer, will you please read this tract?' and I handed it to him. He put it between his fingers, leaned on the end of the rake . . . and I was talking and he was listening." Then Ed realized the man knew no English, but he understood what Ed was saying. Ed was speaking Dutch!

His companion could not believe it when Ed told him what had happened. So a few days later they returned to the house. The man wouldn't invite them in but said he had read the pamphlet. "There were some good things in it," he said, and other things he couldn't accept. Then Ed's companion said, "Well, now, we're missionaries from America."

"I know that. He told me that last week, and you're over here at your own support. You're not taking up collections; you're not selling these tracts."

"No, we're coming to preach the restoration of the gospel," the missionary continued.

"Yes, he told me that. He told me about Joseph Smith, the prophet who he said restored the gospel to the earth and organized the church on the earth today," said the Dutchman. Then the missionary proceeded to discuss the first principles of the gospel. "Yes," said the man, "he told me about that."

"He can't," protested the missionary. "He doesn't speak Dutch. He's only been here for a few weeks."

"Whether he speaks Dutch or not I don't know," countered the Dutchman, "but he talked good Dutch to me and he didn't speak with an American accent like you do."

"It came just like that," Ed recalled, "and left me just like this understanding did this first day. But to me it gave me the feeling, I can learn it. I'm going to try."

After he learned the language, Ed was assigned to be the companion of a new missionary who, when he got off the train, immediately declared that he didn't believe the gospel, that he was on a mission just to satisfy his family and that he wouldn't "get involved in these emotional things" such as testimony-bearing.

It so happened that they had a dinner engagement at the home of a member that night. When they arrived Ed and his new companion learned that little Marietje had fallen against a sharp brick wall and had been paralyzed from the waist down. An operation was to be performed the next day. The girl's mother asked Ed to administer to her daughter. The father held only the Aaronic Priesthood. She handed Ed a bottle of consecrated oil. He handed the bottle to his companion, who said, "I told you I wasn't going to do anything like this."

"That isn't the point," Ed answered. "They think you're a missionary, and you should do it."

146

"Well, I can't speak Dutch anyway."

"We assume God understands English. . . . You go ahead."
He did, and Ed sealed the anointing. "I don't know why I said
it, but I said that she would be healed without an operation.
When I got through and said Amen, she hopped off that couch
and ran into the hall and down in the back. That's the first step
she'd taken since Sunday evening."

To Ed and the family it was a manifestation of the power of
the priesthood. Even the reluctant missionary "gained a little
bit of an insight that there was more to this than just
nonsense."

Following his mission, Ed toured the Holy Land and then
resumed his studies at the University of Utah. One day his
father, who was a bishop and secretary of the George F.
Richards prayer circle, notified Ed that he had been invited to
join the prayer circle. The following week Ed and his father
went to the temple. At the gatehouse they picked up bottles of
oil to be blessed in the temple and later returned them to the
gatehouse where they were sold.

Inside the temple they climbed the stairs to a large upper
room containing wooden lockers with large drawers for the
temple clothes of prayer circle members. They did not take off
their street clothing, but put on their robes and entered the
council room on the west where the Council of the Twelve held
their weekly meetings. Ed was impressed with "those big black
soft upholstered chairs. I had never sat in such a comfortable
chair in my life. The first one was George F. Richards's. If he
was not there then my father, as secretary, was second and
presided. George F. Richards would be in the head chair and if
he were absent it was always vacant."

Following any announcements that Elder Richards might
have, the group of eighteen to twenty men surrounded an altar
"where the list of the ill that we had brought from the
gatehouse . . . would be placed on the altar" and prayers were
offered on their behalf.

On their way to and from the council room each Thursday
evening, Ed noticed, in an adjoining room, the sacrament table
and service used earlier in the day by the Twelve. Occasionally

there were also several large victorian wash basins with tall, plain pitchers, and drying racks with quite a number of white towels on them. The pitchers and towels, he surmised, were used by the Twelve in the ordinance of washing the feet.

When Elder Richards returned from an assignment, he frequently told the circle about his trip. Members "really tried to make you feel welcome; they felt a real brotherhood there," a brotherhood that extended beyond the walls of the temple. For Ed, the prayer circle produced a "very, very good feeling. A strong feeling. I had just come from the mission and this was really a continuation of a fine spiritual experience."

In August 1927 Ed married Hermana Forsberg. They were to have six sons, including two sets of twins. Ed graduated from the University of Utah in education, majoring in history with a minor in philosophy. His first job was teaching history and civics at the Rigby (Idaho) High School. At one stake conference Elder Melvin J. Ballard was the visiting General Authority. When Ed was called to speak, he mentioned that when Elder Ballard had set him apart for his mission, he had promised him the gift of tongues and the gift of healing. Then Ed related his mission experiences, and Elder Ballard responded, "You know, of the hundreds and hundreds of missionaries I've set apart, I have never given anyone else a promise like that. I worried from that day to this because I didn't remember who it was I said it to, but I remember I told somebody that. I often wondered, was he disappointed if it didn't happen?"

The next year Ed was called to teach seminary in Midway, Utah. With many other seminary teachers, he attended the 1929 Old Testament seminar at Brigham Young University given by Sidney B. Sperry, who had just returned from studying the Bible at the University of Chicago. The following year Ed and his colleagues at the seminar were taught by the eminent Biblical scholar Edgar J. Goodspeed.

Ed found Goodspeed to be a brilliant scholar. He opened up new vistas for his Latter-day Saint students. "With Goodspeed you had higher criticism," Ed discovered, "but you had it with a man who had a spiritual outlook, a spiritual background."

148

When the Church Department of Education agreed to help defray some of the expenses for a few seminary and institute teachers to study at Chicago, Ed seized the opportunity. He and Hermana saved what they could and, in 1931, entered Chicago's program in Christian history under the specialist of American religions, William W. Sweet. Among his colleagues who later became important members of the Church education system, were Russel Swensen, Daryl Chase, George Tanner, and George S. Romney.

The classes were very small, and every quarter the professors invited their students to their homes for a social. One night at Goodspeed's home Ed surveyed the professor's library. "Between the book ends there was a King James Bible, the Wescott and Hortt's Greek text of the Bible . . . then there was his New Testament and then next to it the Triple Combination. They were all between book ends on this table there in his drawing room. I was amazed to see that. Somebody said, 'What's this Book of Mormon, Doctrine and Covenants, Pearl of Great Price?' "

"That's a volume of scripture," Goodspeed answered.

Ed wrote his thesis on Orson Pratt, received a master's degree, and began work on a Ph.D. before returning to teach seminary for a year at Rigby. Next came a summer of study at the University of California, Berkeley, and then back to Rigby. The Lyons hadn't even unpacked before word arrived that President Heber J. Grant would be attending stake conference and wanted to talk to Ed.

President Grant called Ed, barely thirty, to serve as president of the Netherlands Mission. "If he had said, 'We're going to send you to Timbuctu,' I'd have been no more suprised," he recalled.

One of President Grant's granddaughters, a lifelong friend of Hermana, gave a farewell party for the Lyons. During refreshments, President Grant turned to Ed and asked, "By the way, Brother Lyon, how old are you?" When informed he was thirty, President Grant said, "Oh, that's good. I'm glad to hear it. I've been criticized for calling you on a mission when you're so young and inexperienced. I'll tell the Twelve when we meet

149

on Thursday that they don't have any reason to criticize me at all. I was a stake president when I was twenty-four and an apostle when I was twenty-six. You're a mission president at thirty. That's getting along in years.''

Ed's four years as mission president (1933-1937) were during the Great Depression, when there were only forty to fifty missionaries in Holland. One of his most important responsibilities was training local leadership to assume duties previously handled by the missionaries. Elder John A. Widtsoe had developed a specific program for this purpose, and the effort was continued when Elder Joseph F. Merrill replaced him as head of the European Mission. Ed wholeheartedly endorsed the program, and gradually transferred Amsterdam, Rotterdam, the Hague, Leyden, Dordrecht, Groningen, Arnheim, Schiedem, Delft, Utrecht and Den Helder to local leadership.

In 1936 the mission celebrated the seventy-fifth anniversary of the introduction of the gospel to the Netherlands. After some difficulty, Ed located the pond where the first baptisms had been performed, had a monument erected, and supervised a centennial pageant in Rotterdam.

When Ed and Hermana attended a mission presidents' conference in Berlin, they got off the streetcar at the wrong stop and, as a result, walked by the chancellory just as the new ambassador from Argentina arrived to meet Adolph Hitler. "He came out on the balcony and stood up there and had all of his elite guard down there goose-stepping, and the clatter of their hobnails on those paving stones was a din." Ed and Hermana managed to work their way up to the fence. When the ambassador got out of his car, "Hitler came out of the door dressed in a pair of striped trousers and a cutaway coat. I never before realized how small he was. He was smaller than all the men around him." The ambassador and the Fuhrer shook hands and walked into the chancellory together as the people yelled and screamed, "Heil Hitler!"

Though he met many Latter-day Saints who opposed the Nazi movement, Ed was distressed to find that some of the Saints were active members of the Nazi Party. Even though the

150

Nazis confiscated several Mormon tracts, a few branch presidents were members of the secret police. Ed was astonished to find a large portrait of Hitler hanging on the wall of the main branch in Berlin opposite a portrait of Joseph Smith. In the evening meeting, one of the brethren preached a sermon on the two great prophets, Joseph Smith, the prophet of the nineteenth century, and Adolf Hitler, the prophet of the twentieth. Ed was disturbed to think any Latter-day Saints could support Adolf Hitler. He realized that fanatical devotion to any political cause could be dangerous.

The Lyons hoped to teach seminary in Ogden when they returned to Utah, but instead, Ed was assigned to be the only teacher at the relatively new Institute of Religion adjacent to the University of Utah. The first year, about seventy students attended his classes at the University Ward. But by the end of World War II the meetinghouse rooms were too small for the numbers attending.

Property was purchased on the corner of University Street and Third South and construction of a new building authorized. "I've never seen a bunch of kids so excited as they were over that new building," Ed recalled. "They held bazaars, they had carnivals, and they raised better than five thousand dollars to buy equipment for the building." Much of the work was done by the students, with Ed and his friend and colleague Lowell Bennion working side by side with them. When the Institute's doors finally opened, the two teachers had 1200 students and nine chapters of Lambda Delta Sigma.

For more than thirty years T. Edgar Lyon was a permanent fixture at the Institute. He taught classes in the Book of Mormon, Doctrine and Covenants, Church history, and other subjects. He participated in devotionals and social activities, and counseled students when they came to him with questions and problems.

Ed might have been satisfied with his reputation as a teacher who established a wonderful rapport with his students. But he was determined to obtain his doctorate. He had selected a dissertation topic, "Evangelical Protestant Missionary Activities in Mormon Dominated Areas," and started research in 1931, but, interrupted by his presidency of the Dutch mission and two summers of study at Chicago, progress was slow. He transferred to the University of Utah, completed courses in history and philosophy, and finished his dissertation. Finally, in 1962, more than thirty years after he received a master's, T. Edgar Lyon was awarded his doctorate.

Widely respected as a Church history scholar, Ed was also a popular speaker at sacrament meetings, firesides, and study groups. He was called upon to write lesson manuals and textbooks for the Church. He wrote articles for newspapers, Church magazines, and professional historical journals.

In the early 1950s Ed met at the University library, and later at the Union Building, with an informal group of university professors playfully nicknamed "the swearing elders." They invited various speakers to discuss the Church and the gospel. "It was an intellectual group," Ed recalled. "They were just trying to get down and explore some things in Mormonism that had been accepted as basic." Among the members were George Boyd, Obert C. Tanner, Waldemar Read, E.E. Ericksen, Sterling M. McMurrin, Jack Adamson, Boyer Jarvis, and William Mulder. Among the speakers were Hugh Nibley, Adam S. Bennion, and Levi Edgar Young. Their gatherings reminded Ed of the nineteenth century "when intellectual groups got together and discussed topics, wrote papers, which were then subjected to criticism and evaluation of the members."

Ed's influence was not limited to Mormons. He participated in several interfaith discussions, and delivered a series of lectures on Mormonism at the Presbyterian church, another series with the Reverend Bill Bremley before the Salt Lake Council of Churches, and yet another series at Westminster College.

During the last years of his life, at an age when most people taper off in their activity, Ed Lyon continued to teach and to serve as the historian of Nauvoo Restoration, Inc. He was anxious to see that the restoration of Mormon Nauvoo be done responsibly and professionally, and not be allowed to become a mere public relations gimmick. An authentic recreation of

Mormon Nauvoo, he believed, would win respect and friends for the Church.

Ed was a charter member of the Mormon History Association and participated in many of its meetings. When the association met at Independence, Missouri, Ed was scheduled to give a paper on the significance of the crossing of the Missouri River, to be delivered on the river bank. Although the wind was blowing and rain began to fall, Ed stood there, bareheaded, and described the early days on the Missouri River. At another MHA meeting he delivered a personal reminiscence entitled "Church Historians I Have Known." Enjoying the friendship and respect of his fellow historians, Dr. T. Edgar Lyon was named president of the Mormon History Association in 1967.

As the leading authority on Nauvoo, he was invited to prepare a volume on the Nauvoo period of Church history for a proposed sesquicentennial series and had compiled impressive files and first drafts of some chapters by the time of his death in 1978.

In all activities, Hermana supported and encouraged him. Both devoted years of time and energy to their family; and when the children grew up and left home, Ed and Hermana continued a close relationship. Recalling how he had fallen in love with her soon after his return from his first mission, Ed said, "I'm still in love with her and I'm still discovering things I never knew possible to be there after all these years, but they're there."

The Church has produced many remarkable individuals who have devoted years of their lives to the seminary and institute program—Franklin L. West, Lowell L. Bennion, Wiley Sessions, George S. Tanner, George Boyd, Ed Berrett, and many others—but no one who knew him would deny that T. Edgar Lyon's energy and devotion as well as his breadth and versatility were unexcelled. His was a unique contribution to the improvement of Latter-day Saint education.

Epilogue

In an attempt to explain Mormonism to his English audience, G.K. Chesterton once wrote, "A number of dull, earnest, ignorant, black-coated men with chimney-pot hats, chin beards or mutton-chop whiskers, managed to reproduce in their own souls the richness and the peril of an ancient Oriental experience."

We appreciate Chesterton's backhanded acknowledgement of Mormonism as a genuine religious movement, but his caricature commits several common errors. First is the mistake, more common in the nineteenth century than in the twentieth, of depicting Mormons as dull and ignorant. While it is true that the advantages of formal education were not available to many early Saints in America and Europe, as well as many modern Saints in today's developing countries, there were and are exceptionally literate and educated men and women who have left us thoughtful diaries and oral interviews reflecting a keen awareness of the world around them and a deep sensitivity to their own experiences.

Next, apparently because he identifies the Church with its ecclesiastical leadership, Chesterton ignores the importance of women in Mormonism—a common oversight that is becoming increasingly recognized.

A third common mistake is to treat Mormonism as a thing of the past. Despite the phenomenal growth of the Church worldwide in this century, even Sydney E. Ahlstrom's recent *A Religious History of the American People* concludes its discussion of Mormonism in the mid-nineteenth century.

In these brief biographical sketches we have tried to give dimension to the vast range of Mormon experience—from the beginnings to modern times, from the uneducated to the professional teacher, from enthusiastic converts to discouraged colonists, from loyal critics to a headstrong rebel. We have seen women as homemakers, pioneers, and innovative leaders. We would like to have included more women, more experiences

154

beyond the Wasatch Front, and more individuals in the largely untapped second century of Mormonism. But there are limits to what can be accomplished in such a short work.

In the hundred-and-fifty-year history of Mormonism, developments within the Church have maintained its relevance in the modern world. Some of those developments can be seen in the lives we have described. But there is also a strong sense of continuity with the past—an abiding commitment to the original religious impulses of Mormonism's first generation. Revelation, priesthood authority, and the implementation of religious ideals in day-to-day living remain the hallmarks of Mormonism. It is certainly much more than "an ancient Oriental experience."

It may be that one of the ultimate values of Mormonism lies in the meaning it gives to the lives of its "ordinary" members—enlarging their vision and enriching their opportunities. We have found that the story of Mormonism is, as the personalities examined in the book demonstrate, the story of extraordinary deeds accomplished by ordinary people.

Bibliographical Note

Except where indicated, all unpublished manuscripts are located in the Historical Archives of The Church of Jesus Christ of Latter-day Saints.

Chapter 1. In addition to Joseph Knight, Jr., "Incidents of History from 1827 to 1844," we have drawn information from the following published works: "Joseph Knight's Recollections of Early Mormon History," edited by Dean C. Jessee, *Brigham Young University Studies* 17 (Autumn 1976): 29-39; "Newel Knight's Journal," *Scraps of Biography* (Salt Lake City: Juvenile Instructor Office, 1883); Larry C. Porter, "The Colesville Branch and the Coming Forth of the Book of Mormon," *BYU Studies* 10 (Spring 1970): 365-85; and *History of Broome County*, edited by H.P. Smith (Syracuse, N.Y., 1885).

Chapter 2. Of special value was the Jonathan H. Hale Journal, 2 vols., and the Aroet Hale Journal, 2 vols. Also helpful was the diary of Wilford Woodruff. See one published portion in "The Kirtland Diary of Wilford Woodruff," edited by Dean C. Jessee, *BYU Studies* 12 (Summer 1972): 365-99. A published biography is Heber Q. Hale, *Bishop Jonathan H. Hale of Nauvoo: His Life and Ministry* (Salt Lake City: privately published, 1938).

Chapter 3. The main sources for the essay on Lyman Wight are: *History of the Church of Jesus Christ of Latter-day Saints*, edited by B.H. Roberts, 7 vols., 2nd ed. (Salt Lake City: Deseret Book, 1964); Lyman Wight, *An Address by Way of an Abridged Account and Journal of My Life from February 1844 up to April 1848* (Austin, Texas, 1848); Marvin J. Hunter, *The Lyman Wight Colony in Texas* (Bandera, Texas, n.d.); Davis Bitton, "Mormons in Texas: The Ill-Fated Lyman Wight Colony, 1844-1858," *Arizona and the West* 11 (1969): 5-26; Philip C. Wightman, "The Life and Contributions of Lyman Wight," (M.A. thesis, Brigham Young University, 1971); and *The Reminiscences and Civil War Letters of Levi Lamoni Wight*, edited by Davis Bitton (Salt Lake City: University of Utah Press, 1970).

Chapter 4. Information for this chapter was gained from the letters exchanged between Thomas L. Kane and Brigham Young. We have also drawn information from the following published works: Norman R. Bowen and Albert L. Zobell, Jr., "General Thomas L. Kane: The Soldier," *Ensign* 1 (June 1971): 23-27; "General Thomas L. Kane: The Pioneer," *Ensign* 1 (October 1971): 2-5; Albert L. Zobell, *Sentinel in the East: A Biography of Thomas L. Kane* (Salt

Lake City: Nicholas G. Morgan, 1965); *The Private Papers and Diary of Thomas Leiper Kane: A Friend of the Mormons*, edited by Oscar O. Winther (San Francisco: Gelber-Lilienthal, 1937); Elizabeth Wood Kane, *Twelve Mormon Homes Visited in Succession on a Journey Through Utah and Arizona*, edited by Everett L. Cooley (Salt Lake City: Tanner Trust Fund, 1974); and Leonard J. Arrington, "In Honorable Remembrance: Thomas L. Kane's Service to the Mormons," *BYU Studies* 21 (Summer 1981): 150-170.

Chapter 5. The main source for this chapter was the diary of Jean Rio Baker Pearce, typescript.

Chapter 6. Leonard J. Arrington, *From Quaker to Latter-day Saint: Bishop Edwin D. Woolley* (Salt Lake City: Deseret Book, 1976), and Preston W. Parkinson, *The Utah Woolley Family* (Salt Lake City: Privately published, 1967) are the principal sources. Also see Minutes of Bishops Meetings, Salt Lake City, 1852-1882; and the minute books of the Thirteenth Ward.

Chapter 7. *The Diary of Charles Lowell Walker*, 2 vols., edited by Andrew Karl Larson (Logan, Utah: Utah State University Press, 1980); and the *Veprecula*, which contains several Walker compositions and verses, were the main sources for this chapter.

Chapter 8. The material for this chapter comes from Lucy Hannah White Flake, Autobiography and Diary, manuscript; and, Roberta Flake Clayton, *Pioneer Women of Arizona* (mimeographed, Mesa, 1969). See also Leonard J. Arrington, "Latter-day Saint Women on the Arizona Frontier," *New Era* 4 (April 1974): 42-50.

Chapter 9. Published information on Edward Bunker and Bunkerville is included in Leonard J. Arrington, Feramorz Y. Fox, and Dean L. May, *Building the City of God: Community and Cooperation Among the Mormons* (Salt Lake City: Deseret Book, 1976); Juanita Brooks, "The Water's In," *Harper's Monthly Magazine*, 182 (May 1941); LeRoy R. and Ann W. Hafen, *The Joyous Journey: An Autobiography* (Glendale, Calif.: Arthur H. Clark, 1973); Elbert B. Edwards, *200 Years in Nevada: A Bicentennial History* (Salt Lake City: Publishers Press, 1978); *The Bunker Family*, edited by Joseph B. Walker (Delta, Utah: Privately published, 1957); and Leonard J. Arrington, *The Mormons in Nevada* (Las Vegas, Nevada: *Sun*, 1979). Unpublished sources are Myron A. Abbott Diary, typescript; Edward Bunker Autobiography, typescript; Bunkerville Ward Historical Record, Bunkerville Ward Manuscript History, Santa Clara Ward Manuscript History, Saint George Stake Historical Record, and Juanita Brooks, "The History of Bunkerville," typescript.

Chapter 10. In addition to the San Juan Stake History, we have used the following published works: Reed W. Farnsworth, "The San

157

Juan Mission," *The Power of Adversity* (Cedar City, Utah: Privately published, 1979); David E. Miller, *Hole-in-the-Rock: An Epic in the Colonization of the Great American West* (Salt Lake City: University of Utah Press, 1966); *Lemuel Hardison Redd, Jr., 1856-1923: Pioneer, Leader, Builder*, edited by Amasa Jay Redd (Salt Lake City: Privately published, 1967); and Charles Redd, "Short Cut to the San Juan," *1949 Brand Book of the Denver Posse of Westerners* (Denver, 1950): 1-25.

    Chapter 11. The main source for this chapter was the 1895 diary of Chauncey W. West. See also Davis Bitton, "Six Months in the Life of a Mormon Teenager,"*New Era* 7 (May 1977): 44-49.

    Chapter 12. We have used the diaries of George F. Richards, Church Archives, and autobiographical sketches by Joel Richards and LeGrand Richards, typescripts in our possession.

    Chapter 13. Sources for this chapter were *Me and Mine: The Life Story of Helen Sekaquaptewa*, as told to Louise Udall (Tuscon: University of Arizona Press, 1969); Grace F. Arrington, "Biography of an Indian Latter-day Saint Woman," *Dialogue* 6 (Summer 1971): 124-26; and an untranscribed oral history of Helen Sekaquaptewa, interviewed by Lamar Helquist, 1 November 1978, copy in possession of Maureen Ursenbach Beecher, Salt Lake City, Utah.

    Chapter 14. The material on Ephraim and Edna Ericksen comes from E.E. Ericksen, *The Psychological and Ethical Aspects of Mormon Group Life* (Chicago: University of Chicago Press, 1922); E.E. Ericksen, "Bendt Jensen Ericksen," and "Ephraim Edward Ericksen: His Memories and Reflections," typescripts in the possession of Edna Ericksen, Salt Lake City. Also valuable were, Scott Kenney, "The Religious Life and Thought of E.E. Ericksen: Crusading Heretic," unpublished paper in possession of the authors; taped interviews with Edna Ericksen, 1973-1981, in possession of Scott Kenney; Scott Kenney, "E.E. Ericksen: Loyal Heretic," *Sunstone* 3 (July-August 1978): 16-27; and various publications of the YMMIA and Primary Association.

    Chapter 15. The material on Margrit Feh Lohner comes from oral history interviews by Sylvia Bruening (August 1972).

    Chapter 16. T. Edgar Lyon, oral history interviews conducted by Davis Bitton, November 1974 to January 1975 provided the major source of information for this chapter. See also T. Edgar Lyon, "Church Historians I Have Known," *Dialogue: A Journal of Mormon Thought* 11 (Winter 1978): 14-22.